CÉLESTE PERRINO WALKER

I
CALL
HIM

Abba

REVIEW AND HERALD® PUBLISHING ASSOCIATION
HAGERSTOWN, MD 21740

The author assumes full responsibility for the accuracy of all facts
and quotations as cited in this book.

All Bible texts, unless otherwise credited, are from the *Holy Bible, New
International Version*. Copyright © 1973, 1978, 1984, International Bible
Society. Used by permission of Zondervan Bible Publishers.

This book was
Edited by Raymond H. Woolsey
Designed by Mark O'Connor
Electronic makeup by Shirley M. Bolivar
Cover photos by EyeWire and PhotoDisc
Typeset: 11/15 Garamond Light

PRINTED IN U.S.A.

04 03 02 01 00 99   5 4 3 2 1

R&H Cataloging Service
Walker, Céleste perrino, 1965-
    I call Him Abba

        1. God—Fatherhood   2. Christian life.
    3. Religious life.   I. Title.
                    231.1

ISBN 0-8280-1345-4

Also by this author:
        Sunny Side Up

To order this book or additional copies of *I Call Him Abba,* call **1-800-
765-6955.**

Visit our website at *www.rhpa.org* for information on other Review
and Herald products.

*This book is dedicated,
with all my love,
to Joshua and Rachel . . .
who call me Mommy*

CONTENTS

THE "AHHH" FACTOR

I was 8 or 9 when I made my first unconscious attempt to have a more personal relationship with God. I was lying on my bed, staring up at the ceiling, praying about something. I started with the usual "Dear God . . . ," and then stopped. I don't remember what I was praying about, but I do remember that I felt I needed to talk to Someone closer than the distant, impersonal "God" I had learned about.

"Dear Daddy" didn't sound right. Then my mind jumped to an often repeated prayer, "Our Father, who art in heaven . . ." God was my Father. I couldn't call Him Daddy. How about Father? Instantly God was someone I had a relationship with, and I felt as though we shared a secret. He was my Father, but He didn't have to go to work every day. He was around anytime I needed Him. To me that was very reassuring.

But, although I have called Him "Father," and later "Abba," since that time, He has still, paradoxically, too often seemed distant, tyrannical, a perfectionist whose standards I cannot hope to meet. No longer a Catholic, I continued to do penance in my own way, hoping to appease Him, hoping that someday He might look down on me and be proud. I never hoped for love, really, just a parental pride and acceptance.

I realize now that the way I looked at God then had a lot to do with how I viewed my earthly father—how I felt about him and how I thought he felt about me. I'm not the product of a perfect childhood. I've yet to meet anyone who is. I grew up feeling that nothing I could ever do would be good enough. But, still I tried, because I wanted to feel that same parental pride and acceptance from my earthly father. I didn't dare hope for what I believed constituted love.

In His infinite wisdom, God gave me time to think about this before He blessed me with my first child. A boy. A rambunctious, in-your-face kind of kid. Unto us a child was born, unto us a son was given, and we called his name Joshua. And one day, not the day he was born but a day farther down the road, I became a mother.

I looked at that child and I thought, *Father, how could You let me love anyone so much?* And that was when I realized how intensely God loved me. Just because I was me. Not because I was anything special. Not because He was proud of me. Not because I had finally beaten myself up enough over my sins. Just because I was me. And when I realized that He looks down on me and says, "How could I love anyone so much?" with that same tightening of the chest I feel when I look at my children, I finally understood what love, real love, is all about.

This book is about the moments I have had since becoming a mother that have helped me understand God and His love more clearly. These are the "Ahhh!" kind of revelations that can be hard to understand before you become a parent. If you are not a parent I hope that you will come to understand, through these experiences, another perspective on how much God loves you. If you are a parent I hope that you will see, through your own children, the depth of God's love for each one of us.

Chapter 1

LOST SHEEP

I TELL YOU THAT IN THE SAME WAY there will be more rejoicing in heaven over one sinner who repents than over ninety-nine righteous persons who do not need to repent. Luke 15:7.

My son, Joshua, was 3½ when he made his first solo hike down to "Dindum's" (his own version of great-grandma) house. You could see the house where Dindum and Pa lived from our back gate; it was probably less than 100 yards. He had to cross the snow-covered meadow, navigate down a hill, and stand by their big silver gate to wait for Dindum or Pa to open it for him.

He wanted to take some of his toys and his blankie, so I packed them into a backpack and strapped it onto his back. It was more bulky than it was heavy, but it made him look ridiculously top-heavy. I couldn't walk with him because I needed to feed his baby sister. So I went with him to the gate and pointed out the way, making sure he listened to my instructions. My heart swelled with parental pride as I watched him set out across the meadow.

He looked a little forlorn as he started out, trudging slowly through the snow. I ran back inside to inform his great-grandparents that he was on his way and to look for him by the silver gate near their yard. Then I took Rachel out of her swing to nurse her. As I settled myself onto the couch I dialed Dindum's house again on the portable phone to make sure he had arrived.

"No, he's not here yet," she reported.

"What do you mean, he's not there yet?" I asked, beginning to panic. "I just saw him go down over the hill. He has to be there by now."

"Well, Pa went out to look for him and he couldn't find him," she said.

I jumped up from the couch, much to Rachel's consternation, returned her to the swing, and raced to the back door. I scanned the meadow for any sight of him, but saw only a boy-less expanse of white. "Joshua!" I screamed, listening carefully for anything, any little noise he might make giving some indication of where he was.

The phone rang. "Pa just came in and he said he couldn't find him," Dindum informed me.

"I'm going after him," I said, hanging up the phone and racing for the door.

I flew through the gate and followed his tracks through the meadow, barely noticing the little sitz spots in the path where he'd fallen down a few times. All I could think was that he must have fallen and not been able to get up, or went too far and ended up down the hill at the barn.

I crested the top of the hill and spotted him, just where I told him to wait. Even at a distance I could see he was crying. "It's OK, it's OK," I yelled, running through the snow. I scooped him into my arms and held him close. My heart raced as a sick feeling invaded my stomach.

I CALL HIM ABBA

The poor little thing had done just as I'd told him. He'd been hollering for his Dindum, and no one had heard him. I wiped away his tears and told him what a good job he'd done obeying me so well.

"Dindum wouldn't come," he sniffled as I opened the gate and helped him into the house.

"Where was he?" his great-grandmother asked as I brought him in, wimpy and subdued from his ordeal.

"Right out by the gate where I told him to go," I replied.

"He was out by that gate?" she exclaimed. "You said he was by the other gate. You should have told me!"

I wanted to say that I had and that she'd misunderstood, but what did it matter really? He was safe and everything was once again OK. Placing blame wasn't going to erase the fact that he had stood outside crying, thinking he'd been forgotten. It wasn't going to still my heart and make the sick feeling in the pit of my stomach go away.

Later, when I'd had time to recuperate from my scare, I realized that if I, a mere mother, reached such heights of panic because my child was missing, how must God surely feel when His children get lost?

I was very familiar with the stories of The Lost Coin and The Lost Sheep, but I had always been most impressed with the quality of patience and determination displayed by the shepherd and the woman. The shepherd goes after the lost sheep "until he finds it." The woman lights a lamp, sweeps the house, and searches "carefully until she finds it." Nothing, however, is said about how panic-stricken they must have felt.

When the shepherd discovers his sheep missing, what is the first thing he thinks? Wolves, bears, mountain lions! Maybe the poor little thing wandered away and fell off a cliff! Maybe it had shattered its leg on some rocks and was suffering! I can't see that shepherd setting off casually in search of his sheep. He runs!

He's out of breath. His lungs are on fire. He's frantic. Where could the sheep be? Is it OK? Is it dead? Is it in pain? Where *is* that sheep?

There!

There it is, caught in some brambles! He frees the sheep and clutches it to his breast, burying his face in the soft wool. His heart threatens to pound its way right out of his chest. His stomach is in knots. A sense of relief and gratefulness floods over him. He's found his sheep.

The Bible doesn't tell us much about the woman who lost her coin, but she must have needed it pretty desperately to search until she found it. Money for her was obviously not easy come, easy go. Perhaps she was a widow and had a limited (if existent) income. Perhaps it was all the funds she had to see her through an undetermined length of time. That coin might have meant food, shelter, goods. It was her livelihood. Without it she could starve.

She searches, on her hands and knees, looking in every darkened corner. She worries, Will I find it? What will I do if I can't find it? I *have* to find it! I just have to! Frightening thoughts of long days and nights without food, slowly starving to death, terrorize her. What will she do? Her light shines just right and . . .

There it is!

She scoops it up and clenches her fist around it. Unconsciously she lets out her breath, not aware she'd been holding it. Her muscles release and she sits back on her heels, slightly shaky, overcome with relief.

I realize now that I've experienced just a little of what God must feel when we wander away and get lost. The one who is lost must surely be glad to be found, but the one who finds him probably had the greater scare. No wonder "there is rejoicing in the presence of the angels of God" when a sinner repents.

I CALL HIM ABBA

Chapter 2

LEFTOVER BLESSING

ESAU SAID TO HIS FATHER, "Do you have only one blessing, my father? Bless me too, my father!" Then Esau wept aloud. Genesis 27:38.

The rocking chair creaked with protest every time I pushed it backward. I wondered why it didn't keep Rachel awake, but she seemed oblivious to everything but my arms. As long as I held her, upright, over my shoulder, patting her back, she was quiet, sometimes drifting off to sleep. But vary that position an inch in any direction and she threw back her head and began to wail.

To say that my arms ached after hours of this routine would be an understatement. I discovered muscles in places I didn't even know I had arms. At 17 pounds, Rachel was no lightweight, and I was getting tired. Rob, who would have spelled me, was sick too. Tonight I would have to go it alone.

As her breath caught in muffled half-sobs she burrowed her face against my neck, trying to clear her nose, which was clogged up from a cold. I could feel the heat radiating from her. The poor little thing felt miserable. One by one, different arm muscles went numb, and finally I was forced to change positions.

I pushed myself off the rocker, trying not to disturb Rachel, and began to pace up and down the hallway again. Motherhood had developed in me a peculiar bouncy walk whenever my arms were wrapped around a baby, and Rachel and I bounced our way up and down the hall. At one point I thought she might actually go back to sleep, but when I tried to lay her down . . .

"Waahhhh!"

Up we went again for more bouncing. She hiccupped half-hearted cries into my ear, and I nuzzled her soft head, murmuring comforting words such as "Rachel, please go to sleep. I'm exhausted." And "What is *wrong* with you? I know you're tired."

But I knew what was wrong with her. She had her first cold. I didn't know what was wrong with me. How could I be so impatient with her? Patience with Joshua had been a point of pride with me until he turned 2 and learned how to push all my buttons. Rachel wasn't even 5 months old yet.

I slumped against the bed and slid down, rocking and cooing. I'd already sung a few dozen renditions of every lullaby I knew, and it hadn't helped. Rachel had considered it fine entertainment and joined in with a meandering *"arrgggghh-hhrrrrgggghhh"* in conversational tones that I presume were meant to be accompaniment. As I thumped her gently on the back she "talked" to me, but all I could think of was the sleep I was missing. It was 2:00 in the morning, and we'd been at this since 11:00 at night after I had finished work for the day.

I was exhausted.

Even so, my lack of patience concerned me. Joshua had been an extremely hard baby, and although I had never possessed much patience before I became a mother, I was the very

I CALL HIM ABBA

definition of patience with him. I was patient through the first four colicky months while he was demanding and irritable, and nothing I did could please him. I was patient as I rocked him to sleep night after night while he screamed like a banshee in my ear over the sound of the vacuum cleaner we turned on to soothe him. I was patient when he woke me up again and again nightly for two years to nurse.

When I became pregnant again I was counting on the old adage that if you have two children they will be completely different. To ensure my survival they *had* to be completely different. No way could I imagine going through what I did with Joshua all over again.

As much as I loved Joshua—and I loved him fiercely—I couldn't imagine loving another child as much. And yet I did. From birth Rachel seemed to go out of her way to make life easy for me. She let me get more sleep than any new mother had a right to. She was easy-going and happy. I caught her first smile on film when she was two days old. At a week and a half she laughed out loud.

And yet here I was treating her with less patience than I gave to perfect strangers. It was as if the cup of my patience had been emptied by Josh and there wasn't much left for Rachel.

I know of one man, a father, who felt the same way I did. His name was Isaac and, presumably, he had just given his blessing to Esau, the elder of his two sons, the one who was his favorite. When he found out he had been tricked into giving his blessing to his youngest son, Jacob, he was mortified.

Too late! It was too late to call it back.

Esau cried, "Bless me—me too, my father!" But Isaac's cup of blessing was empty. He had poured out his best. All he had left for Esau was a parody of the blessing he had given to Jacob. Esau got the dregs, the sediment in the bottom of the cup.

LEFTOVER BLESSING

Sometimes our best gets away from us.

That night I could hear Rachel cry, "Be patient—be patient with me too, Mom!" But I wasn't. Oh, my arms were patient and my back was patient, but my heart was not patient at all. Every time she cried I wanted to put her down in her bed and run so far away I couldn't hear her.

When Joshua asks me to play with him and he hears, "Not now, Josh, I have to nurse the baby," or "I can't play right now, I have to work. Maybe later," I can hear him cry, "Pay attention to me—pay attention to me too, Mom!" And I can't.

Although my best is often distributed in uneven proportions, I am confident that someday I will learn how to dispense it with more wisdom. I will learn how to give my best to both children. My cup of patience will run over.

But I'm thankful that my Parent gives me and each of His other children all of His patience, all of His attention, all of His blessing, all of the time. We don't have to wait. His firstborn Son's name was Joshua also, but we know Him better as Jesus. He received all the blessing and honor and love a firstborn usually receives. His birthright included paradise.

And God said, "This is my Son, whom I love; with him I am well pleased."

When we, His other sons and daughters, came along, God could have given us second-best. He could have given us the leftover blessing. Instead He gave us everything. He blessed us with all He had given to Jesus and more. He sacrificed Jesus, His firstborn, for us so that we can be with Them both in paradise. Now that's what I call being richly blessed.

Rachel shifted in my arms. Her limbs stopped flailing, her head rolled slowly to one side. Finally, she was asleep. I laid her down on the bed and—amazingly—she continued to sleep.

For a few hours.

Chapter 3

CIRCUMCISION

THE LORD YOUR GOD WILL CIRCUMCISE your hearts and the hearts of your descendants, so that you may love him with all your heart and with all your soul, and live. Deuteronomy 30:6.

Dr. Bernstein laid out his gleaming instruments on my grandmother's kitchen table right next to the "circumcision board," a flat plastic contraption with indentations that looked as if a baby had been pressed onto it before the plastic had hardened. There were small Velcro straps to hold down the baby's arms and legs. It looked more like an instrument of torture than medical equipment.

This wasn't the first time I had ever seen such a board. As a naïve 18-year-old nursing student I had done a rotation on the maternity floor. There had been an identical piece of equipment in the nursery. I had always kept it on the peripheral of my vision, not willing to look at it directly and therefore acknowledge not only its existence, but its purpose. But I knew what it was for.

During my rotation there had been only one circumcision. The doctor performing it had forbidden the nursing students to attend, even though we were supposed to observe procedures. Barred from the nursery, we had milled like restless cattle out by the nurses station, glancing skittishly at the closed door of the nursery from which issued the most piercing screams.

That was almost 15 years ago, but practices hadn't changed much. I clutched my 9-day-old son and sashayed away from the board. "Do you have to use that thing?" I whimpered piteously.

Dr. Bernstein paused and gave me a once-over, probably thinking *Oh, great; another squeamish mother who's going to get in the way.* "Well, you could hold him," he said, "but it's much safer if we strap him in."

"What about an anesthetic?" I pleaded. "Can you give him an anesthetic so he won't feel it?"

Dr. Bernstein pulled on thin surgical gloves with a snap that made me jump. "I could," he admitted. "But that's a shot at the site." He looked pointedly at me. "And then we'd have to wait for it to take effect, about five minutes. He'd scream the whole time. In my experience, it's better to just get it over with. It takes less time and is less traumatic to the baby."

I cringed at the word "traumatic." Circumcision hadn't been an easy decision to begin with. We hadn't even thought about it until Lamaze class. Our instructor told us that the local doctors were against it and performed "partial" circumcisions.

The other mothers-to-be in our class really didn't have an option. But because our baby was going to be born at home, if it was a boy I was going to have to find a doctor who was willing to perform the procedure either at home or in his office. I had to drive an hour and a half from home, but I located a doctor who was willing to perform a traditional circumcision at the home of my grandparents, who lived nearby.

As I handed my chubby little baby over to be strapped onto the evil-looking board, I wondered if maybe I should change my mind. Dr. Bernstein placed Joshua in the baby-body depression and strapped his arms and legs in place. Even though he was only 9 days old, Joshua looked for me and screamed.

The entire procedure took less than five minutes, but it was agony for me. I felt as limp as a dishrag when it was all over, and I wanted to snatch him from the doctor. The rest of the experience was a blur of trying to nurse my inconsolable child, listen to the doctor's instructions, and quiet my racing heart.

I would sooner have gone through labor again (all 27 hours of it) than repeat the experience.

I think Zipporah probably felt the same way. Although the Bible doesn't give us much of an account of her experience, I can imagine how she felt. With her husband's life threatened she had no impartial doctor to turn to who would perform the procedure for her.

It was a matter of life or death. She took the flint knife in her hand and bent over her baby, her firstborn. Quickly she unswaddled him. Maybe he began to cry, maybe she did too, but she couldn't stop. The baby squirmed, his cries turning to screams, and her heart seemed to freeze. For a moment, I imagine, she wondered if she could actually do it.

And I'm sure Zipporah would rather have relived every moment of her labor, too, if it would have saved her from that awful experience. The moment it was done I know she scooped up her baby and rocked him back and forth as her tears stained his bare skin. Her arms wrapped around him, her soothing words promising him safety, begging forgiveness for the hurt. His body would be stiff, sobs wracking his tiny frame.

We go through the same thing. God, our Father, promises to circumcise our hearts. His scalpel is circumstances—trials, we like to call them. Murder, loss, theft, cancer, illness, betrayal, incomprehensible crimes. Our misfortunes and the misfortunes of those we love seem so senseless. We stiffen and scream, "God, where are You? Why is this happening?"

And God sobs, "It's OK. I'm here. I'm right here."

Circumcision hurt my son. I know that. But his circumcision hurt me most of all. Twenty minutes after it was over he slept peacefully in his grandmother's arms. Nearly four years later I still break into a sweat just thinking about it; he doesn't even remember.

Sometimes I think that if I hear just one more horrible story of abuse, injustice, or murder, my sanity will snap. Right now, these things seem larger than life itself. In the last year alone, I lost my grandfather and nearly lost a grandmother. Members of our immediate family suffered one separation and two divorces. Serious health problems have stalked several family members. Rob's work screeched to a near halt just before Christmas.

When tragedies hit close to home they can be particularly devastating. What we have to remember is that looking back from eternity the pain of this life will be just a dim memory for us.

But God will break into a sweat just thinking about it.

Chapter 4

SHARING THE PAIN

AFTER HE DROVE THE MAN OUT, he placed on the east side of the Garden of Eden cherubim and a flaming sword flashing back and forth to guard the way to the tree of life. Genesis 3:24.

Thinking back on it later, neither Rob nor I could figure out what had prevented us from hearing what must have been a horrible banging. All we found was the evidence of the dirty deed: Joshua's new bat lying next to his big Tonka bulldozer. The top of the dozer was caved in, squashed flat as though Goliath had sat on it while pondering the cowardice of Israel. But the marks on the bat pointed to a more realistic and depressing cause.

I was on the phone when Rob stumbled on the scene of the crime, but even that didn't prevent me from quickly figuring out what was going on. "What is this? What happened here? **Joshua!"**

When I got off the phone Joshua was seated forlornly in time-out, and Rob darkly beckoned me outside to view the heinous crime. "Look what he did," Rob said. He rotated the bat so I could see all the marks. Although it was a metal bat, it looked as though the Babe had used it, and used it hard, for half his lifetime. The dozer was equally sad looking. "What should I do?" he asked.

We had been planning to get ice cream in celebration of Mother's Day. Josh was extremely excited about that because he was just getting over a cold and had had almost no desserts for a week. My heart sank as Rob continued. "I think he should be spanked, and he shouldn't get any ice cream."

It wasn't even my punishment, but I nearly burst into tears.

"What do you think?" he asked. "Do you agree?"

By virtue of having read nearly everything ever written on children I am the resident child care expert, and Rob usually confers with me on the tough ones. This one, in my opinion, was too tough.

"I don't know," I whispered. "I guess so." Suddenly I didn't want to go out for ice cream at all. I gathered up the baby and nuzzled the soft downy hair covering her head. Why did kids grow up and do stuff like this? Why couldn't they just stay innocent and happy? Why did there have to be discipline?

From Josh's perspective this was going to look arbitrary and unjust. Chances are he would get the message about destroying things, but he would probably not recognize the love behind the discipline for many years to come. Part of what broke my heart was knowing that he would think of us as ogres until he was old enough to realize what love, true love, was and how it expected the best from you and wouldn't allow you to harm yourself without trying to stop you.

I waited while Rob explained to Josh that because he had ruined his bulldozer with his bat he was going to be spanked, and although we were still going to get ice cream he wasn't going to be able to have any. After cringing through his spanking, we soberly filed into the car and headed out.

Ben and Jerry's is probably five miles from our house, but it was the longest, most miserable five-mile drive I have ever made. Every moment I was aware of Josh's broken sobs and weak sniffles. I think he half expected us to relent. *I* half expected us to relent, but one look at the stubborn clench to Rob's jaw let me know that relenting wasn't an option.

"Can I have some ice cream?" Josh asked me hopefully as I unbuckled his seat belt.

"No, honey, you smashed your nice bulldozer, remember?" I replied, fighting back my own tears as he renewed his.

Getting ice cream that day was much more of an ordeal than a treat. Rob ordered an ice-cream cone, and I got a sorbet that I shared with Rachel. We ate them in glum silence as Josh sat watching, just outside our usually cozy, close family circle, in the place he had removed himself to.

As I watched him that day it was not hard to picture another scene. I could imagine the gray haze of a chilling fog clinging to the earth outside the gates of Eden as two miserable people clutched each other for solace. Moving slowly away from the entrance, they eyed, perhaps a little fearfully, the angel who guarded the entrance to what had so recently been their home. Seeing tears staining the golden face of One whom they had conversed so happily with about the garden and the animals did nothing to ease the great burden of guilt they felt at having disobeyed God.

In the flash of the cherubim's sword, the newly acquired pain they could see etched in each other's drawn faces must have seemed as foreign as the land they now walked on. If not for that flashing sword I have no doubt they would have turned headlong and thrown themselves back into the garden, pleading for mercy. Fear clutched their hearts. They felt abandoned and alone.

But they weren't.

God sobbed on the other side of that gate. Perhaps bent over a rock, as Jesus was in Gethsemane, His face pressed against the cold stone. His salty tears anointed the rock. The air echoed with His cries. His hoarse voice threw a thin reedy wail into the cool night air as gut-wrenching sobs shook His shoulders.

Heartbroken, He experienced their punishment as if it was His own. He endured the separation that *they* had chosen, and He made plans to restore them at *His* expense. God didn't simply sit back to watch our little history play out. He became vested in the drama. He suffered right alongside Adam and Eve as they stumbled out of the garden to find a place to dwell. He is with Joshua in the ice-cream shop. He is with me when I lose my temper. He is with each of us as we pull away from Him.

Adam and Eve removed themselves from the garden because they *chose* to disobey. God received their punishment, but He did nothing to deserve it. And that is how a parent suffers with a child.

Children who do much more than dent bulldozers with bats cause their parents' hearts to writhe in agony. Children who run away, or kill someone while driving drunk, or divorce their spouses and split up their families because they tire of them. The parents of these children will suffer as if they had performed the deed themselves. Because that is the nature of parental love. You cannot love someone, truly love someone, without being affected by the things that they do.

"My son, do not despise the Lord's discipline and do not resent his rebuke, because the Lord disciplines those he loves, as a father the son he delights in" (Prov. 3:11, 12). Though they may sob on the other side of the gate, parents have a responsibility to correct their children even as they hurt with them. And it can be the hardest thing they have to do.

Chapter 5

IS NOTHING SACRED?

CHRIST REDEEMED US FROM THE CURSE OF THE LAW by becoming a curse for us, for it is written: "Cursed is everyone who is hung on a tree." He redeemed us in order that the blessing given to Abraham might come to the Gentiles through Christ Jesus, so that by faith we might receive the promise of the Spirit. Galatians 3:13, 14.

My midwife's office was in an old house painted light blue. A doctor's office occupied the first floor. Gravel crunched under my feet as I made my way around to the side door that opened onto a steep staircase. The stairs smelled like old vitamins, and signs for "holistic" health care were thumb-tacked onto a bulletin board lining the small space. I climbed the stairs, feeling panic expand in my chest. The note on the door said to knock, so I did, and a cheerful voice called, "Come on in."

The midwife walked across the small room to meet me. She was dressed like someone you might meet at a health food store—baggy, natural-fiber clothing, and Birkenstock-style sandals. She wore no makeup, and her long, straight hair was drawn back in a simple ponytail. There was not one thing about her that put me in mind of medical personnel. Before I could speculate on whether I was willing to place my first pregnancy and the life of my unborn baby into her hands, I became aware of the room.

It was small but accommodated two couches, two wicker chairs, an old desk, and an examining table that was covered in cloth to make it seem less threatening. A bursting bookcase leaned up against one wall. Next to that was a toy box burgeoning with much-used toys. A rubber plant and a table with boxes of herbal tea and some mugs were set up against the opposite wall. The walls themselves were covered with pictures. They were filled with photos of mothers and babies of every shape and size. There were pictures of mothers breastfeeding, giving birth, in labor, and about every situation in between, wearing, for the most part, nothing more than a smile or a grimace of pain.

It should have dawned on me then, but thankfully it came much later—motherhood was the beginning of a series of losses. The first thing I lost was my dignity.

It's impossible to remain dignified when your breakfast comes back up quicker than it goes down. Or when, in spite of that, you gain enough weight to qualify as a small country. The process of being in labor and giving birth itself doesn't allow for the merest shred of dignity. And breastfeeding, no matter how adept you are, is not exactly dignified, either. I now have pictures in my personal photo album that resemble those I saw at my midwife's.

With the advent of my baby, other losses followed in quick succession. The first thing to go was sleep and personal time. I lost exercise and devotions. I lost hobbies and work. When my

I CALL HIM ABBA

child grew up and began to get into things I lost order and cleanliness. I lost my temper and my patience. I lost my personal possessions, because everything qualified as a toy. Josh would clamor to look through my treasure boxes.

One by one he opened them—the carved one, the shell-covered one, the black-lacquered Oriental one, the brass one—and examined the contents: motel stubs from when Rob and I eloped on Valentine's Day, pennies squashed by a train, candy Valentine hearts Rob gave me on that first Valentine's Day, my favorite marble when I was a kid, some coarse tail hair from my first horse. Chubby, clumsy fingers broke and lost things that were precious to me.

There was nothing sacred in my house. It didn't matter to Josh's curious nature that my scissors belonged in the drawer by the kitchen sink so I could find them the next time I needed them. He did not care that the papers on my desk were organized and shouldn't be written on or thrown around the room. My favorite mug made the same *clunk* when he dropped and broke it that any other mug would have made. If he drew on the arms of the couch with permanent marker it made no difference to him.

Having a second child only increased my losses. Most of the time I feel completely poured out to fill the needs of my demanding little family. There is nothing of me left, nothing held in reserve. All of it is given, every second of every day.

And yet what I have gained has filled me so full of love, pride, accomplishment, and gratitude that it is impossible to regret what I have given away. My losses are barely noticeable next to the incredible amount I have received.

I went into parenting not knowing what I was going to lose and what I was going to gain, but God entered parenthood knowing full well what it would cost Him. He lost the beautiful world He had created when Adam and Eve sinned. He lost the companionship of His children, as well as their respect and love. And His Son's dignity was stripped by a birth of questionable legitimacy, a life of abject poverty, and a death of base ignominy, which also reflected on Him. He lost His Son to their greedy hands, forever to carry the scars of their disobedience.

Nothing He has is sacred to us. We trample on His law, His name, His earth, His word, with equal insensibility. With words from the same language we praise His name and curse it. We break His Sabbaths with as much thought as we break promises. We manipulate, use, and destroy His created works, His children, according to our needs.

And yet, in our simple faith we fill Him up. Our prayers, our love, our hope in Him makes every sacrifice pale into insignificance. Jesus will not hold out His hands to us and point at the scars, saying, "See what I did for you? See what you cost Me? I went through agony for you." He loves us so much that He gave everything, even His life, freely, willingly. He knew exactly what love would cost before He gave it, and He offers it still.

That is love. The "wide, long, high, and deep" love that He has for us. It is God's sacred love that surpasses all knowledge and cannot be changed, altered, or destroyed, no matter how hard we try.

Chapter 6

GOD'S TIME-OUT

BUT THE LORD PROVIDED A GREAT FISH to swallow Jonah, and Jonah was inside the fish three days and three nights. Jonah 1:17.

I press limits every day. Of endurance. Of patience. Of busyness. Of relationships. Today, will they bend? Will they break? What will happen if I push them to their outmost boundaries? I test them, sometimes gingerly, sometimes without regard to the consequences. There are moments when it just doesn't matter what the outcome is.

When I've been up all night with a sick child it doesn't do any good to remind myself that my health requires a good eight hours of sleep or it will begin to break down. Pushing the limits of my energy is not my choice. I'd much rather kiss the children on their sweet, soft, rounded cheeks and send them off to play while I dive under the covers for 40 or 80 winks.

When my life is spinning out of control and exhaustion threatens to overwhelm me, my time with God slips away practically unnoticed. Suddenly I realize I miss Him. It's been awhile since we talked, and I feel distant from Him. Hey, yeah, when *was* the last time I sat down and spent any time with Him, anyway? Has it been *that* long? Ouch! I didn't mean to push that limit, either.

And then there are times when I push the limits on purpose. When I deliberately take time to relax instead of spending it with God. Or when I take on another job that will rob the people in my life of my time. It's those times when I feel like Josh when he tests me. At 2, he liked to test his limits—and mine. To him the word "no" was a challenge, a gauntlet thrown. It didn't stop him; instead, it spurred him on.

One summer day, having just toddled down to the mailbox with me, he was playing in the kitchen while I prepared lunch. As I chopped carrots I glanced over the countertop in time to see his hand reach out to pull the stack of mail down on his head. My voice, laced with warning, impeded him. "Joshua!"

A grin touched his lips. His fingers inched closer to the mail. I shook my head, assembling my features into a stern arrangement. "Joshua, leave the mail alone."

Giggling, he grabbed the edge of the bottom envelope. I knew what I had to do. With motherly determination I shook my head firmly. "No, Joshua."

He grinned and pulled. Down fluttered the mail.

"Time-out," I proclaimed, wiping my hands on a dish towel hanging from the fridge. I walked over to him, sitting happily on the floor surrounded by mail. Scooping him up swiftly, I deposited him into the chair we used for time-out. Bending down to eye level, I caught his small impish face gently between my palms so I could look directly into his eyes.

"Joshua, look at me. Mommy said no. When Mommy says no, she means no. Do you understand? Now I want you to sit here for a few minutes and think about what you did." I cranked the dial on the kitchen timer and set it on the table beside him. Then I returned to my lunch preparations, watching my son out of the corner of my eye.

Joshua squirmed and he wiggled. He tried whining angrily in protest, and sliding half off the chair, his legs dangling over the side as though he might make a break for freedom. He did everything but quietly accept his punishment.

Tick-tock. Tick-tock.

Two minutes was forever.

Finally the buzzer went off, and I helped him down from the chair. "I love you, Joshua," I told him, enveloping him in a hug. "And I want you to grow up to be an obedient boy. Are you sorry for disobeying Mommy?"

He nodded. "Yes."

"Give Mommy a kiss." He promptly planted his sticky lips on my cheek. "Let's ask Jesus to forgive you." I helped him clasp his hands together and he bowed his head, mimicking me. "Dear Jesus, please forgive Joshua for disobeying Mommy. Help him to be an obedient boy. Thank You. Amen."

"Ah-men," Joshua echoed. I kissed his soft cheek and ruffled his hair as he scampered off to play.

Time-out was supposed to accomplish a number of things. Provided that the location chosen for time-out was sufficiently devoid of interesting or stimulating items, it served to make the recipient anxious not to make a return trip. The time spent in time-out gave kids a chance to reflect on the behavior that got them there in the first place. It also gave them time to cool off and experience repentance.

I know that's what Jonah did.

The word of the Lord came to Jonah and he ran off, instead. He'd take a boat; yes, that's what he'd do. He'd head in the opposite direction from where God wanted him to go.

He'd go so far that God could never find him. Never, ever, not in a million . . .

Then a storm came up and terrified the crew of the ship. They prayed to their gods, they threw cargo out to lighten the ship, then they cast lots to find out who was responsible for the storm. And guess who it turned out to be? Poor Jonah.

Ploop!

Into the drink went Jonah. And God, not having a kitchen chair handy, sent a big fish to swallow Jonah. Time-out.

Drip. Drip. Drip.

Seconds ticked off like eternities in the smelly belly of the fish. And Jonah grew very remorseful. Oh, I know how he felt. I have experienced God's time-outs. Plowing along on my own steam, all-the-stops-out, no-holds-barred, winner-takes-all, when suddenly everything goes wrong. It pulls me up short. And I sit kicking, squirming, and frustrated in the kitchen chair of my life, thinking about what got me there in the first place.

I was all set. Things were going my way. And that's usually the problem. They were going *my* way. At some point along the line things had stopped going God's way and the focus of my life had shifted to me and what I wanted, not to God and what He wanted. And sometimes, like Jonah, I want to run away from God and what He wants. But you can't run away from God. He can put you in time-out no matter where you are.

"My son, do not despise the Lord's discipline and do not resent his rebuke, because the Lord disciplines those he loves, as a father the son he delights in" (Prov. 3:11, 12). So, the question then becomes, how do we respond to God's rebuke? The answer depends on where our priorities really are.

Have you experienced a time-out in your own life? Have you run up against a wall, asking "What next, Lord?" Frustrated plans, lack of communication, dry seasons in our lives are all

God's way of trying to get our attention. When we barrel ahead, intent on our own pursuits, He is right behind us like a toddler's mother, ready to reach out and grab us by the suspenders and plunk us in time-out.

But He doesn't abandon us there. He's with us in our time-outs. He didn't abandon Jonah, and He won't abandon us either. We may not hear Him in our busyness or our frenzy, our meetings or our commitments. We have to listen. That's why He often brings us to a place where there is nothing left to do *but* listen.

ICHA-2

Chapter 7

THIS THING CALLED DEATH

THE LORD GOD MADE GARMENTS OF SKIN for Adam and his wife and clothed them. Genesis 3:21.

When I was growing up, we lived in the country, in a log cabin (how quaint); my parents were into self-sufficiency. We grew a lot of our own food, raised our own meat, and generally did as much as possible ourselves. (Maybe I should explain at this point that I did not grow up Adventist.) So I was introduced to this thing called "death" early on.

My induction was hastened by the inopportune arrival of a batch of baby bunnies. After several attempts at raising rabbits it had been discovered that the male rabbit had to be removed from the female's cage or he would eat his own offspring. And so, one bright spring day when I was maybe 8, we had our first successful litter of baby bunnies.

Maybe it was childish exuberance, maybe just plain naiveté, but I did not expect that we would ever, ever *eat* our fluffy little playmates. I'm not sure that my mother planned it that way, either. But this was a couple years before the log cabin and the country, and we had no room for extra pets. So my mother, with Yankee frugality, packed us all into the car one day, along with the rabbits, to visit Mémère Gagné, her mother.

It was a long trip, nearly an hour, which is a lifetime to a child. I don't remember wondering what was going to happen to the bunnies. I was probably more interested in speculating on whether or not any of my uncles would be busy with chores in the big dairy barn. My Aunt Marie was fond of taking us into the hayloft, along with a jar of bubbles that we would blow down on the unsuspecting boys as they did their chores. It was an exciting and fun game.

But when we got there Mom told us to stay in the car. She and Mémère Gagné took the bunnies into the garage. My sisters and I waited uneasily, not understanding what was happening, not liking the terseness of the situation. I had the car door open to get some air, and to my horror I saw a stream of blood running from inside the garage down the driveway and past the car door.

"Mom? What's happening?" I called fearfully.

"You know," she replied. "We're butchering the rabbits. Now, stay in the car."

I don't suppose she gave it a second thought. Growing up on a farm it wasn't unusual to be sent out to the chicken coop before dinner with the request to bring back the guest of honor. She learned at an early age to single-handedly butcher and dress the bird. With a large family to feed there wasn't much time wasted on squeamishness.

But for me, eating an animal that you used to cuddle was a new experience, and I didn't like it one bit. Every time rabbit was served (and later chickens, pigs, sheep, and goats) eyes widened and appetites waned. Who could eat a main course that used to have a name?

Joshua's first pet was in no danger of being eaten. Besides the fact that we are vegetarians, none of us would have even considered eating a hermit crab. The consensus was unanimous. We'd rather eat shoe leather first.

"Look at his cute little eyes," Joshua cooed. He was 3 years old and had lots of knowledge gleaned from books about sea life of every conceivable, and often inconceivable, kind. "Look at his cute little claw. Oh-h-h-h! He's pinching me!"

Despite their rocky start, Josh soon had Hermes accustomed to riding around in the palm of his hand as he showed him his toys, took him on field trips, and tried to get him to eat things. I think the crab liked it.

Josh was quite a responsible pet owner for a 3-year-old. Most of the time he remembered to put food in Hermes' shell dish, and soak a piece of natural sponge that Hermes used as a water bowl.

But sometimes Josh dropped Hermes. Or put him on the table or sofa and forgot him; later we would find Hermes scuttling across the floor. If the cover wasn't put on his makeshift home Hermes would drag the piece of sponge to the side of the container and climb up and over, making his escape. Unfortunately, the container was kept on a wooden table about two and a half feet off the ground. Over the edge Hermes would walk, completely unaware of the danger, then *plop!* onto the floor.

Being a mother and therefore paranoid, I began to live in terror of Joshua accidentally hurting Hermes. What if he pulled his claw off? Or what if someone stepped on him? Or what if Josh dropped him and he died? There were a lot of things to be afraid of in a relationship between a small boy and a very small hermit crab. And the more attached Joshua got to Hermes the more worried I became.

And then one day it happened.

"Mom," came his quavering voice one morning as he

checked on his pet. "Mom, Hermes' claw fell off."

"What?" I shrieked as calmly as I could. "What do you mean, it fell off?" Immediately I feared the worst. He'd pulled Hermes' claw off. Could a crab live that way? Were there veterinarians for crabs? I tried to get control of myself. I used to be a nurse. I could handle this.

I peeked into the container. There was Hermes, strangely still. Next to him was his one big claw. Normally when we opened his container, Hermes withdrew into his shell. This time he didn't withdraw. He didn't even move. I picked him up. Hermes was most certainly dead.

"Oh, Josh," I said softly.

"What?" he asked, worry clouding his eyes.

"I'm afraid Hermes is dead," I whispered.

Joshua broke down in great, gulping sobs and I held him, patting his back. This was one hurt I couldn't kiss away. There was nothing I could do to ease the pain of experiencing death for the first time.

I imagine that when the beautiful creatures on the earth began to die, God felt the very same way. Handing Adam and Eve the skins of the first animals slain to provide for them a covering, He must have wept deeply for the innocent life cut off. And He knew there was more to come. So much more to come.

I suspected that Josh had something to do with Hermes' untimely demise, but we later found out that it was because of a lack of humidity that he died. Not so with God. As He observed death up close and personal He didn't have to wonder if perhaps Adam and Eve were responsible. He *knew*.

Down through the ages, from Cain to Ted Bundy, the deaths would multiply. And Adam and Eve, tragic couple, how they wept when they realized the enormity of what they'd done. Death was for a lifetime, and this was only the first one they had experienced. It had become, in the space of a single decision, part of living.

The people in Josh's life rallied around him with their sympathy. Of course, we immediately replaced Hermes with a new crab, which helped a lot. And our friend Rich Edison composed this poem for him:

Ode to Hermes

A crab's crab was Hermes.
One big claw and a little one too.
He loved to play and scuttle about.
Sometimes he'd even hide from you.

Never a crab to waste a word,
He showed his love by just staring
Shy and not much for show,
A shell was the fanciest thing he'd be wearing.

A great crab he was
and he'll be missed, 'tis true.
But soon you'll laugh again,
because here comes Hermes Two!

When Hermes Two, also known as Soup, was killed accidentally by a visiting pooch during Joshua's birthday party, Josh took the crab's death much more philosophically. And I couldn't help but be disappointed that already he was becoming hardened to death, accepting it as the natural order of things.

Because it is *not* the natural order of things, as I'm sure God must have told Adam and Eve as they mourned over Abel's body. This time I think they must have understood. Yes, they would die, but if they claimed the promise of a coming Redeemer then that death would not be eternal. It would be a pause between this life and the next. And in that life our Creator God will make all things new.

Chapter 8

PICTURE PERFECT

SEE, I HAVE ENGRAVED YOU on the palms of my hands. Isaiah 49:16.

There were childless years when I filled the photo holders in my wallet with pictures of my dogs. The collection of heart frames on my bureau had only furry faces staring lovingly out at me. I never went so far as to hang up pictures of my dogs on the walls, but there was a gold locket-type Christmas tree ornament with a place for pictures that has Rob and me kissing at the altar on one side, and my wolf-hybrid, Kävik, on the other.

Since the birth of my children my camera has worked overtime to capture their images on film. I am as determined to record every minute detail of their lives as I am afraid that I will miss an important stage of development and have no permanent record. I have pictures of my children in my wallet, on my walls, on my refrigerator, in square plastic photo holders on my keychain, in their baby books, in my mother's journals, on bureaus all over the house, and countless photo albums.

Most of the time I try to dress the kids in their best clothes before I take their pictures. I comb, curl, fuss, tease, and fight with their hair to get it to do *something* presentable for the camera. I prop them up or stand them in a photogenic area where the wallpaper won't suck the color from their faces or an unsightly mess distract the viewer from the main object of the photo.

Most of the time I succeed, and the pictures I get are priceless, just what I was shooting for. But there are other times when I get even more impressive photos without even trying. A boy racing an ocean wave can't be staged. A baby, moments old, covered in the fluids of birth can't be cleaned up first. Spontaneous moments can't be manipulated, but they can be captured.

Nursing Rachel yesterday, I happened to notice a photo I took of her at Christmas. She is bending intently over a wooden puzzle of safari animals. On her head is the catching end of a bug net. It used to be Joshua's, and then it broke. Always creative, he used it as a helmet when playing David and Goliath. For some reason Rachel also preferred it as the headgear of choice, and would often ask to have it placed on her head while she toddled around.

She is also wearing a red-and-white-striped playsuit. Normally I don't dress her in red, pink, or any derivative color because it is particularly unflattering to her complexion. But this outfit was in the 25-cent bin at the local secondhand clothes store, and it still had a lot of wear in it. I just couldn't pass it up.

This picture is displayed on her bureau even though she couldn't have been dressed more hideously if I had outfitted her on purpose. So, what is it doing in a place of honor? I studied the photo and decided that it was there not because of how

Rachel was dressed, or even that she'd been placed in an exceptionally photogenic spot.

It was there because of the intense look of concentration on her face as her tiny fingers reached out to pinch one of the knobs on a puzzle piece and wiggle it out of its position. It wasn't on her bureau because it captured anything special on the *outside* of Rachel. It was there because it captured something of the *character* of Rachel.

I like to think that God has similar pictures of us on His walls, in His wallet, or on His refrigerator. They aren't pictures that capture us as we present our best face to the world, all polished up with our best clothes on. They aren't there because we are stationed propitiously in front of the Grand Canyon or another spectacular scene. They are there because they capture us in a moment of time that means something important. Our birth as a Christian. Our first joyful awakening to God's imprint in Creation. The moment we learn to put our focus on Jesus rather than on ourselves.

"You see there?" God will point triumphantly, a smile of parental pride on His face. "That one is My favorite."

"But he has mud all over himself," the viewer will protest. "Why, he's filthy. You can hardly even see his face, and his clothes are totally ruined."

"Yes," God will say, "but that was the exact moment when he learned to lean on Me and let Me lead him."

"But what about this one?" the viewer will argue. "Surely there can't be any worth in this picture. The texture is grainy. You can't even make out her features. And the place around her is disgusting. It looks to me like she's a . . ."

"That one," God will reply, "is one of the best pictures in My collection. That one is of My daughter Mary. She loved Me very much. That picture was taken the night she decided to follow Jesus and give up her life of sin."

Spontaneous moments. They may not make a perfect picture, but then the images in a photograph are most meaningful to the one who took the picture. Each captures a moment in time that will never be repeated. And each is worth a thousand words.

Chapter 9

SCHOOL OF
HARD KNOCKS

WHICH OF YOU, if his son asks for bread, will give him a stone? Or if he asks for a fish, will give him a snake? If you, then, though you are evil, know how to give good gifts to your children, how much more will your Father in heaven give good gifts to those who ask him! Matthew 7:9-11.

It's hard going through life banging your forehead on closed doors trying to open them. It's rough doing things backward because no one ever showed you how to do them the right way. Or you were too afraid to ask. I recognize this. That is why I struggle to spare my children the same agony I experienced when I was growing up. It usually sounds something like this:

"Joshua, honey, no. You should leave your new turtle here in the car because if you drop it in the ocean it will be lost forever. Do you understand what I mean? If you drop it you'll never find it in the ocean, and then you won't have your nice turtle anymore."

"But, Mommy, I want to bring it into the water with me. I promise I won't let go of it. I'll hold on to it real tight."

"Josh, it's not a good idea."

"Please, Mommy, I want to bring him swimming in the ocean."

"Well, OK."

Ten minutes later:

"Wa-h-h-h-h!"

"Joshua! What's wrong? Did you cut yourself on a shell?"

"My turtle! I dropped my turtle, and the ocean swallowed it! Wa-h-h-h-h-h!"

Saving someone else from learning painful lessons rarely works. I rather suspect that most of the world's geniuses didn't take someone else's word for things. They tested them out for themselves. Even if the lessons were painful they allowed themselves the opportunity to learn something that the previous person didn't learn. I'm not claiming to be a genius, but in many ways I'm like this, even though it was not always by choice.

I like to say that I graduated from the School of Hard Knocks and got a degree in persistence from Tough Luck U. It's a pretty accurate statement. Not that I wouldn't have taken advice from those wiser and more experienced than myself. The problem was that when I needed advice no one would give it to me, or I was too timid to ask for it.

I am a first child (also known as the oldest). We're the ones who usually become leaders because we are self-starters. Many times this happens because when we are young our parents have another baby and we are somewhat—I won't say neglected, it's not that—but we are left to fend for ourselves a little more. And we are encouraged to set a good example for our younger siblings. We are given responsibility early, and not usually indulged as much as the "baby" of the family. A lot is expected of us.

We butt our heads against anything that doesn't move or make sense. We never take anything at face value, particularly if we think we can improve on it. And if you can't figure something out give it to us because if we can't, we'll work on it until we can take it apart and put it back together again in our sleep.

We question everything. It's in our nature.

I never questioned God, though. Or I should say I never questioned the *existence* of God. I questioned Him plenty of times. I reached a point where believing in God wasn't enough anymore. I wanted it to make some difference in my life. I challenged God to show me that believing in Him changed me somehow. That it gave me power I didn't have without Him.

Too often, we aren't bold enough asking God for power. When we don't seem to be connected to Him we fail to question Him to find out what the problem is. If there's a cord missing from us to the Power Source we ought to be demanding to know where it is so we can repair it immediately.

We have this right. Paul declares, "Let us then approach the throne of grace with confidence, so that we may receive mercy and find grace to help us in our time of need" (Heb. 4:16). How can we ever get what we need if we don't ask for it? Timidity will get us nowhere in this life.

My Mémère Gagné lived on a farm and had a new house built that had broken pieces of glittery mirror pressed into the big chimney, and other "modern" marvels that thrilled our childish eyes as we watched the house erected. My sisters and I would occasionally spend a few days with her and that's when I remember seeing it.

I was walking behind the new house and there, under some eaves, carelessly discarded, was a huge, wooden dollhouse. My Pépère Gagné had probably made it for one of my aunts, and they, having outgrown it, left it outside to the mercy of the elements.

How I wanted that dollhouse!

During the remainder of my stay I envisioned the things I could do with it if only it were mine. I plotted ways to ask Mémère if I could have it. I psyched myself up and prepared little speeches I could give, outlining the reasons why she should allow me to take it home.

In the end I was too chicken; I never asked her if I could have it.

As the years passed, I watched it slowly rot into the ground, because I had been too afraid to ask for it. Every time I think back on that dollhouse I kick myself for not having had the courage to ask my grandmother for it. She probably would have given it to me gladly, happy that someone would enjoy it once again. Of course, I'll never know.

It was difficult for me to understand at that time that there is no such thing as a stupid question. And the only question you ever regret is the one you didn't ask. God encourages questions, because He has answers for them all.

He's just waiting for us to ask.

He even wants us to ask the difficult questions. He wants us to reach down inside, to the place where no one else is welcome, and find the questions that really hang us up. He even wants those questions. Because those are the answers that will change our lives.

Like a parent, He is eager to save us from learning through hard experience by patiently teaching us. He can help us to see in the darkness of ignorance. We don't have to stumble around in the dark, because He will show us the light. He will give us the hand we need to cling to. The kind of hand that lets us reach into places where we can't reach by ourselves.

I CALL HIM ABBA

"Joshua! What are you doing?"

What he was doing was obvious. He was perched up on top of the kitchen stool, teetering precariously while he reached into one of the top cupboards for something. I raced to him and threw my arms around his legs.

"Be careful! Do you have it? OK, get down. I've got you."

When we reach beyond ourselves God is there too. He grabs us around the legs and holds on while we grasp something far removed from our own puny range.

"Be careful! Do you have it? OK, get down. I've got you." And we, flushed with excitement, claim our prize while we are secure in the arms of our heavenly Parent.

Chapter 10

WAY TOO SELFISH

A VOICE IS HEARD IN RAMAH, mourning and great weeping, Rachel weeping for her children and refusing to be comforted, because her children are no more. Jeremiah 31:15.

The desk in my bedroom is essentially a table, but I chose it for its rough hewn boards and simple lines, not its functionality. It doesn't have any drawers or cubbyholes. No shelving unit makes it utilitarian. No sliding keyboard shelf makes it high tech. It's just an old farmhouse table. I like the way the wood feels to my hands and the strength of it as I lean on its top and stare out the open window to watch the morning unfold as I spend time with my God.

And I liked that time. I cherished it and I guarded it jealously. Over the years I've discovered that solitude and quiet, thoughtful periods are vital to my sanity. I may joke a lot about liking to be alone because I'm my own best company, that no one listens to me the way I do, but the truth is that without a lot of time to reflect, my brain just spins in fruitless circles. It's during the quiet moments that the Holy Spirit can really speak to me, when He has my full, undivided attention.

Imagine the disruption, then, that a squalling eight-pound baby boy caused. As he grew, the peace of our house was quickly shattered by childish shrieks during games of tickle-hide-and-seek and loud, off-key renditions of "The Wise Man Built His House Upon a Rock." During the past five years that wise man has built whole cities of houses. Little feet thundered on the hallway floorboards as a small body pelted into Mom and Dad's bed for a morning cuddle. Temper tantrums and laughter, sobs and squeals, echoed through our house at all hours. And as the years progressed they multiplied rather than diminished.

Rachel added a new level of noise to our home. And just like people who live by the railroad tracks grow so accustomed to hearing the trains that they don't even notice them after awhile, we became accustomed to the volume of our house. *It got to be normal.*

In the first blush of new parenting, even jarring realities such as unaccustomed noise pale in significance to the marvel of new life. Watching a tiny baby grow is the most awesome gift of creation that we can behold. In the act of bearing and raising children we can draw close to God and experience something of His magnificent power in creation. We can take part with Him. It is one of the closest experiences we can have with God.

Of course, it doesn't *always* seem that glorious.

While I was on the phone with a friend one day and simultaneously changing a dirty diaper, we got on the subject of kids, and I asked him if he was ever going to have kids.

"No way!" was his emphatic response. "I'm way too selfish to have children."

His answer jarred me. I have never considered myself particularly unselfish. How was it that I was coping so well with children?

I gave that question a lot of thought. My conclusion was that it didn't have so much to do with my disposition as it had to do with my love. I loved my children, ferociously. I wanted what was best for them. It was only natural to put their needs above my own. It was self-sacrificing, perhaps, but it was self-sacrifice motivated by love, which is really no sacrifice at all, but an act of love.

And then something happened that put it all into perspective. One day, before Rachel came along, Joshua went with his grandparents to visit some relatives for a couple hours. I wandered anxiously around the house, wondering what was wrong, unable to put my finger on it. Finally I realized that it was *too quiet*. The lack of noise, of activity, was unsettling.

I wondered where he was. If he was having fun. If he was warm enough. If he missed me. When he was coming back. I couldn't concentrate on anything long enough to make it worthwhile. Finally I gave up and took to pacing and tidying up, listening with one ear for the crunch of tires on the gravel. Those few hours lasted an eternity.

I imagine the Garden of Eden must have sounded the same to God when Adam and Eve were banished from it. Their laughing voices, so content and joyful, were gone. The animals prowled restlessly, searching for them like a faithful dog whose master will never return. They sensed something was wrong.

God wandered pointlessly along the paths He had trod such a short time ago in the company of His creations. Everything reminded Him of Adam and Eve, who had pulled His hand, tugging Him to this or that, asking what it was or how He had thought of it. There was nothing in the garden that didn't remind Him painfully of their close and special friendship.

He wandered over to the entrance of Eden, nodding

solemnly to the angels standing guard with their flashing swords. They marveled at the tears streaming down His face as He gazed mournfully down the path Adam and Eve had taken in their exodus. He could still see their faint, dusty footprints in the sand, leading them away from Him and from their home.

And even today He is still listening anxiously for the crunch of gravel on the driveway outside, telling Him that His children are finally home. Because once you love someone that much, your life never seems complete without them, no matter how much noise they make.

Chapter 11

GRATITUDE ADJUSTMENT

ALL DAY LONG I HAVE HELD OUT MY HANDS to a disobedient and obstinate people. Romans 10:21.

It was a long, hard drive after a tiring, but fun, week visiting friends. I had taken the kids and gone to visit my bosom buddy, Sandy, in the next state. Rachel was young enough to still have trouble sleeping through the night, particularly away from home. I averaged three or four times each night staggering from my bed to soothe and nurse her. Rob stayed home to work, so I had been managing the children without any help. That might not have been so bad had Sandy and I not stayed up late every night, gabbing and careening through cyberspace, pretending we were teenagers again. Somehow stunts like that catch up to you when you're 30.

The road seemed endless. It wasn't long before one blonde and one bald head were sagging against the side cushions of their car seats. I gratefully plugged in a tape and settled down for the monotonous drive. As I neared Quechee Gorge I suddenly remembered that on the way over to San's we had passed a place where Josh likes to ride a little train. At the time we couldn't stop, so I had promised him a ride on the way back. A peek in my rearview mirror confirmed that he was still fast asleep.

It was probably due more to thinking about how I would have felt as a child to have missed out on a treat than the reality of how Josh would feel about it that made me pull into the parking lot. I was patting myself on the shoulder, congratulating myself on being such a perceptive and self-sacrificing parent; I would be missing an hour of child-free driving on the way home.

When Josh woke up he wasn't in a particularly good mood, but I chalked that up to after-nap grouchiness and trundled the kids inside to buy tickets for the train ride. It had just pulled out and we would have to wait another 15 minutes before it was scheduled to leave again. Josh was still whining and crying, saying he didn't want to ride the train. Now he loves this train, so I endured his protests and bought us maple pops to suck until the train arrived.

Besides, I knew what was best. He was going to enjoy the train once we were actually on. I was sure of it. As it chugged out of the station his whimpers would turn to smiles. Guaranteed.

His whining got worse.

I was at a loss. I had the tickets in my hand, and Yankee frugality forbade me to rip them up, pack the kids in the car, and go on home. But was it really any use to drag a whining, pre-temper-tantrum child onto a train and risk ruining everyone else's time?

That's when I got angry.

I was doing him a *favor*. I was giving him something he had begged for. I was being *generous*. And he was hurling my gift right back in my face. Not only hurling it, but stamping on it with impudence. He didn't want it. Or, at least, he didn't think he wanted it. The result was the same. I was experiencing rejection—*from my own child.*

Parents give to their children. That's what they do. It's not even a conscious thing. We give to them from the moment of conception and it isn't until they deliberately reject our gratitude that we even realize it. And kids can be very ungrateful to the people who love them most.

So can we.

Peter did it without even flinching. For years he had rubbed shoulders with Jesus. He ate with Him, walked with Him, laughed with Him. He heard the message up close and personal. He was one of the disciples, the "children" of Jesus. One of the flock.

Then one night Jesus wrapped a servant's cloth around His waist, took a basin of water, and reached out to cradle Peter's dirty, grime-encrusted feet in His hands. Peter recoiled, indignant. "What do You think You're doing? You're not going to touch my *feet!*"

"But if I don't, then you won't have any part with Me," Jesus replied sadly. He knew this was just the beginning of 24 hours' worth of rejection. Peter was only indignant now. Later on he would be cursing. Because he didn't want a part with Jesus. Not really. Not if it meant being arrested with Him at the Garden. Not if it meant being identified with Him before everyone in the high priest's courtyard. Not if it meant suffering ill rather than good for God. No, sir.

So what if he *had* said, "Then, Lord, not just my feet but my hands and my head as well!" He changed his mind later.

And don't we all?

"Oh, Lord, Thy will be done," we cry, but when it is, we reject it. Like cranky children we don't even recognize His blessings when they shower down on us. We just run for our umbrella. Because sometimes blessings come in disguises that we don't recognize, and then we think that God doesn't know what He's doing. Or we figure He's punishing us for something we did.

That's probably how Josh felt. *Mean old Mommy,* he probably thought, *making me go on an old train ride. I'd rather be in the car going home instead of here in this old place, licking a maple lollipop and riding on this dumb old train.*

Haven't you ever thought that way? *Mean old God. He knows I hate this job. I've begged Him to help me find another one and I'm* still *stuck here. Why is this happening to me? I'm not going to grow any this way.*

That was me, once upon a time. And I felt a little sheepish when later I found that the very skills I had detested learning helped me to become a writer. Because no writer is simply a writer; he or she is also a business person. Working those tedious years, learning office management skills, honed business competence in me that enabled me to make my writing a successful business.

There are blessings that just don't look like blessings, no matter how hard we look. That's why we have to trust God. We have to trust Him so much that we follow Him without questioning. Only when we soften our hearts and stop whining in rebellion will we be able to relax and enjoy the ride.

Chapter 12

MY LIFE CHANGED ON FIRST BASE

FOR THE LORD TAKES DELIGHT IN HIS PEOPLE; he crowns the humble with salvation. Psalm 149:4.

It was a beautiful October day in Vermont. The last good weekend of the year, they said. The kids at church had been wanting to play softball all year, and this was their last chance. It had been about 15 years since I had played softball, but I went to help them make up the numbers so they could have enough people on each side to play a game.

In the warm-up, Kevin, the pitcher, asked me where I liked the ball. "Right on the bat," I shouted back. "And if you'd like to save some time, you can just turn around and throw it into the outfield, 'cause that's where it's going, anyway."

We had big kids and little kids and in-between kids and middle-aged kids pretending to be on the neighborhood softball league again. We ran all over the field. Some of us to cover massive gaps and some because we couldn't remember which position we were supposed to be playing.

As our team got slaughtered I remembered what "team spirit" felt like. I didn't care so much if we won, but closing the gap would have been nice. As I raced around the bases, time seemed to be spinning backward. This was every softball game I ever played as a kid. As I crossed homeplate the sand puffed up and dusted the catcher. Home!

After six innings my body tried to remind me that this sort of thing might have been OK in grade school, but anyone past puberty shouldn't push it quite so hard. As always, I had no time to listen to my body. It was my turn at bat and I was going to go home again. I cracked the ball and headed for first base. Out of the corner of my eye I saw the pitcher catch the ball and throw it to first just before I got there.

I landed on first base with my left leg and felt my knee completely blow out. My momentum carried me onto my right leg, but I could not bring my left leg forward and fell flat on my face. I writhed on the ground, hyperventilating. My teammates thought I was laughing.

"Who's up next?" someone shouted.

I went home, all right. Via ambulance and the emergency room.

"Don't walk on it. No weight-bearing whatsoever. Here are some crutches. Here's a brace. Elevate your leg. Use ice. Take a painkiller and follow up with an orthopedist."

At home, Mom being flat on her back holding down the couch got old real fast.

"Why do I have to help?" Josh whined as he stomped around helping Rob move anything that wasn't bolted to the floor so that I could maneuver on my crutches without breaking my neck in addition to my leg. "It's not fair. I've got to do everything. Why can't Mom do it?"

"Look, we've all got to help out until Mom feels better."

And on and on it went.

I learned what it was like to ask for an ice pack or a glass of water and have to wait for it. Trapped on the couch, I had a new perspective. I had lost my independence on first base, and from where I was sitting it was not a pleasant view.

Flat on my back, I acquired a little more empathy for my children's seemingly unending demands. When you can't do much for yourself you tend to demand a lot. And you are easily frustrated when you are put off over and over again. It's easy to bark about having patience but much more difficult to practice it.

I imagine Saul had some experience in this department. When he climbed onto shaky legs on the road to Damascus and shook the dust off his robes it must have surprised him to find that he couldn't see. Not so much as his hand held in front of his face. The man who led mobs had to be led by the hand. Oh, the humiliation of accepting the help of others when you are a self-sufficient leader. The horror of helplessness.

In a room at Judas' house on Straight Street, Saul struggled to understand what had happened and why. As the sun marched from one horizon to the other each day his frustration grew more and more intense. Frantically he probed the future. Life as a blind man was unthinkable.

He might have heard Judas' wife downstairs, complaining about having to take care of him. "Did you have to bring him *here?* Haven't I got enough to do without taking care of a blind man?" Accepting kindness from unwilling hands would only have made his helplessness that much more unbearable.

He didn't eat. He didn't drink. But he prayed. Oh, how he prayed. Gut-wrenching "Why?" prayers. Why me? Why this? Why now? Sometimes it takes a lot of looking to see why. Sometimes it is right in front of us. And sometimes we just never see it. For Saul, it happened in a vision when he saw a

I CALL HIM ABBA

man named Ananias come into his room and lay soothing hands on him. They were confident hands, strong hands, and then he could see! He could see!

Not just with his eyes, but with his heart as well. His vision had cleared up. His skewed perspective gently replaced by heavenly hands like the lopsided hat of an overly energetic child. With renewed energy and a fresh outlook he was ready to take on the world.

When God wants to get your attention, your life can change on first base or on the road to Damascus. It doesn't really matter. What is important is the fact that you can dig past the pain to uncover the lesson buried like a treasure in the middle of the suffering. Because there is always a lesson, and discovering it makes all the difference between growth and self-pity.

My children have discovered what it's like to have to pitch in a little and do things for themselves and even for me. And I have learned to have more patience with little people who can't do things for themselves. We all have to make allowances for each other when we are at a disadvantage. Every time we take the lesson to heart we come that much closer to home plate.

Chapter 13

LABOR PAINS

A WOMAN GIVING BIRTH TO A CHILD has pain because her time has come; but when her baby is born she forgets the anguish because of her joy that a child is born into the world. John 16:21.

I was in agony. I had been like that for hours. All through the night my body strained to expel my first baby through the birth canal and into my waiting arms. But it was not to be an easy labor. Chest deep in a horse trough full of water that my midwives had set up in my bedroom, I groaned and then screamed my way through contraction after contraction. Each of them gripped my body with cruel, relentless fingers of pain.

My midwives spelled each other, taking turns coaching me through the contractions. Toward morning a soft summer rain fell on the porch outside. Nancy sat on the chair in front of me as a contraction rippled over my abdomen, and I shifted to try to move away from it before finally accepting that there was no escape.

"That's it," Nancy soothed. "You're doing great. Your baby will be here in no time."

I looked up at her with eyes that, if they reflected the despair in my heart, were dull with fatigue and agony. What she said meant nothing to me. I couldn't grasp the fact that soon I would be holding a baby, *my* baby, in my arms. It had been years since I'd baby-sat, much less held a newborn in my arms. It didn't mean anything to me. At that moment I would have traded 100 babies for one pain-free minute.

"I changed my mind," I panted. "I want a puppy."

The pain was unending. I could vaguely remember the beginning, but I couldn't pinpoint the exact moment in time when it had become so all-encompassing that everything else ceased to exist. The contractions pelted me like the fists of a seasoned boxer. There was no respite. Even the dawn brought no relief from the continuous pain of the night.

Repeated reassurances by my midwives that the baby would be here soon and the pain would be quickly forgotten did not raise my flagging spirits. Twenty-seven hours into labor I couldn't remember being pain-free, and I had no real hope that it would ever end. There is a time when pain becomes so intense it colors your thinking. You reach a stage when you cannot imagine your life without it. As far into the future as you can stretch your imagination you see yourself enduring your current agony.

And then it happens.

There is a small glimmer of hope, shining like a tiny torch at the end of a long, dark tunnel. "I can feel the head," Laurie announced. "You should be able to birth it in the next push."

Immediately I felt relief. My spirits, which were flagging hopelessly, rebounded at once. The end was in sight! The pain would soon be over! It was incomprehensible, but I grabbed hold of the faith I placed in my midwife and channeled all my energy into pushing.

LABOR PAINS

Moments later when I held the squirming, slippery bundle of new life in my arms the pain was instantly gone and forgotten. It happened that fast. My sister, who had born no children at the time, asked me to describe the contractions afterward and I couldn't do it. I couldn't really remember what they had felt like, just that they had been painful.

Eve knew, because God told her in the garden. There would be pain with childbirth. But pain was a new experience. Who could say if this was normal? It felt as though her body was being compressed by enormous, harsh hands. Was this what God had been talking about? Or was she dying at last as He had said she would? Was there any sense in this agony?

Every moment we are alive we are being pushed through a heavenly birth canal. It isn't easy for us, and it isn't easy for God, either. The pain women suffer during labor, those terrible body-wrenching contractions, massage and stimulate the baby as it passes through the birth canal so that it will breathe well on its own after birth. The pain has a purpose. And so does our time here on earth. It's preparing us to live in heaven with God, who will forget the pain of being in labor the moment He gathers us into His loving arms.

When a woman finds out she is pregnant one of the first things she does is to ask all of her friends who have had children exactly what labor is going to be like. And, of course, there is no answer because pain of any kind is indescribable and all labor is different. But there is one thing that all pain has in common.

It grants us empathy. True empathy. No one can understand where you are coming from when you are hurting so much as a person who has been there. That was one reason why my midwives were so effective in coaching me and my husband was not. They'd been there. They could empathize. They knew what it felt like.

When we have pain here, when we're low and downtrodden, we can know that God knows *exactly* what we're going through *because He was here too.* Jesus suffered worse than the most miserable of us. He can empathize. He knows what it's like.

And when we've passed through to the other side of the tunnel and step out into the light, with our pain and suffering behind us for any given experience, we can't just walk away from it. That experience will go along with us; it will be a part of us forever. We have inside us empathy for those suffering like we did. It is part of our ministry to comfort those who suffer as we have. Because we can empathize. We know what it's like.

It's one of the good things about pain. "And we know that in all things God works for the good of those who love him, who have been called according to his purpose" (Rom. 8:28). Part of that good, a part that can be birthed only during the bad stuff, is this empathy. It's like a passport into the lives of hurting people. It gives us license to tell them that this life is just labor. It won't last forever. Soon we will be birthed into life eternal, where no one will ever suffer for a moment, and the pain of this life will be just a dim memory when we are enfolded in the Father's arms.

Chapter 14

A HANDFUL OF LEAVES AND HALF-DEAD FLOWERS

ALL OF US HAVE BECOME LIKE ONE WHO IS UNCLEAN, and all our righteous acts are like filthy rags; we all shrivel up like a leaf, and like the wind our sins sweep us away. Isaiah 64:6.

It's not one of my best childhood memories, which probably explains why it's stuck with me so long. Our minds have an amazing capacity to retain the bad even more than the good. I was maybe 6 or 7 years old, and I had been coloring. None too well, probably. But I wasn't really as interested in the quality as I was in the project. I was coloring a picture for my dad.

He was in the den working on some kind of electrical gadget, for his job, I think. I was pretty proud of my picture when I brought it into the den for him. I hesitantly approached the desk where he was engrossed in lots of mysterious wires, circuits, and things, and handed him the picture.

"Look, Dad. I made this for you."

He looked at it briefly. "You can do better than this," he said. "Look, you colored outside the lines. You're supposed to stay inside the lines. You have to take your time."

The sad part is that I can't remember ever coloring another picture for him.

It is so easy to become discouraged when you offer a gift to someone much bigger and more powerful than yourself. Your whole being is wrapped up in their reaction to your gift. If it is welcomed, your self-esteem receives a boost of energy. If it is scorned, little bits of your self-esteem, your self-value, are chipped away, leaving you damaged. Sometimes permanently.

Gift giving, particularly when the gift is something that you created, is a delicate matter. It is an intimate act, and it makes you vulnerable. One way or another, it can change your life.

I can't remember now what was upsetting me. I just recall sitting on the edge of my bed, crying. I know it had been one of those days. The kids had been particularly uncooperative. The house was on the verge of being declared a national disaster area. The dogs had been underfoot, either scratching on the door to go in or out, barking for water, or having to be chased home from the neighbor's. It was just too overwhelming.

Sitting there with my arms wrapped around my knees, staring at the wall through my tears and trying to get a hold of myself, I felt a tap on my shoulder. Then Josh's soft voice saying, "Mommy, I picked you these."

A fistful of colorful leaves, recently blown to the ground by harsh fall winds, and what had to be the last of the flowers in my flower garden, mostly dead, appeared in my field of vision, clutched in a grubby hand. It certainly wasn't the most beautiful bouquet I had ever seen. Chances are no florist would even classify it as an actual arrangement. But it was the most beautiful thing I'd ever seen.

I pulled Joshua into my arms and cried even harder. "Thank you, sweetie."

A HANDFUL OF LEAVES AND HALF-DEAD FLOWERS   65

Mary knew what it was like to offer a gift, the best that she had. And she didn't even do it privately, where rejection would have been much easier to handle. Quietly, she moved into the room. Hugging the wall and wishing she could melt into it, she skirted the edge of the cluster of men around the table, who were oblivious to all but the table talk. In her hands was an alabaster jar filled with nard, a perfume made from the aromatic oil of a plant grown chiefly in India. It was a gift so rare and fine that she trembled inside at the very idea of offering it.

On the one hand she could imagine Jesus' happiness at receiving such a gift. On the other, what if He didn't like it? She couldn't bear considering that. But she was determined. She would give her gift and take her chances. One way or another, it would change her life.

Silently she crept up behind Jesus. The alabaster jar was meant for a single application. She took the sealed flask and broke the long neck, spilling the perfume onto Jesus' feet. Using her long hair, she wiped the oil from His feet. The aroma of the perfume broadcast her deed instantly to the entire room. There was no going back. Now it wasn't simply between her and her Lord. Everyone knew.

"What did you let her do that for?" Judas demanded shrilly. "That's expensive stuff. Look at it! All over the floor and You reek with it. It'll take You weeks to get rid of that smell. And think of the cost! That money could have been better spent on the poor."

Mary cringed. This was just the sort of response she had expected in her heart, and she writhed in mortification. Her face burned and she let her hair drape forward like a curtain to shield her from their accusing stares.

Expecting a rude shove or to be manhandled out of the room, her heart jumped when she heard Jesus' soft, warm voice. "Leave her alone. Why are you bothering her? She has done a beautiful thing to Me."

A beautiful thing!

The words rang in Mary's heart. Her gift had not only been accepted, it had been appreciated and valued, as she had been valued. She lifted her head and allowed her hair to fall away from her face so she could look up into Jesus' eyes. She saw love and gratitude. Emotions that powerful are impossible to hide.

It's easy to be intimidated by gift-giving. We've all had experiences where our best efforts have been rejected or not appreciated. Presenting the works of our hands to God, many of us approach Him trembling and anxious. We know that nothing we do could ever be impressive to the One who created the universe and all that is in it. No matter how much effort we put into it, nothing we do could ever repay our debt of gratitude to Him. And we creep up and lay our gifts at His feet, hoping for His approval, His acceptance.

But God doesn't accept our gifts because they are anything special in and of themselves, any more than Josh's handful of leaves and dead flowers were the bouquet of my dreams. He accepts them because they are gifts from His *children,* and He knows that if our hearts could give the gift we want to give it would put all earthly florists out of business.

No matter how poor our attempts, no matter how inadequate our gift, His words are always the same: "Thank you. You have done a beautiful thing to Me."

Chapter 15

CREEPY CRAWLIES

FOR BY HIM ALL THINGS WERE CREATED: things in heaven and on earth, visible and invisible, whether thrones or powers or rulers or authorities; all things were created by him and for him. Colossians 1:16.

I hate grasshoppers.

Not so much because they're ugly, although they are. Not really because they hop in any direction without any warning, though they do. And not even because they have prickly little feet that cling very tenaciously to whatever they land on—and give me a shudder when it happens to be my leg or arm or hair they decide to use as a landing strip.

No, the reason I hate grasshoppers is because when I was a little girl I was walking out to the meadow behind our house, minding my own business, when suddenly something jumped inside my pant leg and began scrambling around. I hopped frantically, shaking my leg and screaming in decibels that are normally reserved for shattering glass.

Doors up and down the block opened with loud crashes as wondering parents and kids poked their heads out to see what the ruckus was all about. My mother flew out of our house and reached me in bounds that would have done a kangaroo justice. Before the eyes of curious spectators she ripped my pants down to my ankles and extracted the culprit, one very large, very ornery grasshopper that immediately hopped away for less hysterical pastures.

The critical situation being over, my mom helped me to pull my pants back up, and I slunk toward the house to see if I could outlive the embarrassment of the situation, or failing that, to lay plans for becoming a recluse. But I never forgave that grasshopper or any of its relatives for the humiliation I suffered because of them.

My hard feelings have had a profound effect on my life, even though I little dreamed that they would. Because my first child was a boy. A real boy's boy. A boy who loved every creepy crawly thing on the face of the earth. If it had fur on it, that was OK, but if it had scales or warts or slime, that was even better! The worse it smelled or looked, the better he liked it.

Watching him one day, collecting bugs and slugs, I realized something. He has had experiences that I have never had and, moreover, have no intention of ever having. He knows things that I don't. He knows how grubs feel between your fingers. He knows what grasshoppers feel like when they cling to the back of your hand. He has had toads chirp in his hand. And he *enjoys* those things.

Each morning the summer sun warms up mercilessly as it climbs the sky and already the hum of insects sounds loud in my ears. It's only 6:00 in the morning, and I hear the door slam, making me roll over with a groan. He's gone again. It happens every morning.

"He's gone outside," I whisper sleepily.

"I used to be just like that," Rob moans before he falls back to sleep.

Joshua's childish squeals drift in through the open window as he finds some icky, sticky treasure buried under a rock or log. Sometimes he collects them in the dog bowl (the dogs never seem to mind), sometimes in a sand pail that will smell a bit raunchy later on at the beach. He always brings them inside around breakfast time to show off. Like a proud pet owner at a show.

"See this one, Mom? Isn't he a big, slimy one?"

"Oh, yes, big and very slimy," I agree.

"Look, I found some grass for my toad to eat. Do you think he likes grass? I found him under the same board this morning. I'll let him go later. Doesn't he chirp nice? Look at this fat grub. Isn't he big?"

I can't say I do more than suffer squeamishly through his escapades with the creepy crawlies. I don't begin to approach a state anywhere near actual enjoyment. But his delight in them is contagious, and I don't have to relish the feel of them in my own hands to experience that.

One of my favorite photos of Josh shows his 2-year-old, still very babyish face lit up with delight as he studies the biggest slug I've ever seen. Rob discovered it on a canoe camping trip we were on, and the two of them were fascinated by it. I stuck to a safe position behind the camera and let them enjoy it together, happy to share without an actual hands-on encounter.

And I think there are some things that God will experience only through me and you. He created every baby born on earth, but He has never held one still attached to its umbilical cord and warm from the womb. He's never been married and known what it feels like to have your husband come up behind you when you are working and knead strong fingers into your neck muscles to rub away the cobwebs. He's never passed a test that He was afraid to fail. He's never done anything horrible and had to ask for forgiveness. And He's never felt the rush of relief when all is made well again.

If things had gone the way He planned, these things wouldn't thrill us, either. We all would be living carefree lives, free of sin and its effects. Our babies would be born without pain. Our neck muscles wouldn't get sore. We wouldn't have to take tests. And we would never, *ever* do anything we needed to ask forgiveness for. This old world is a far cry from God's best intention for it.

Yet He is so good that we can always find some beautiful thing to treasure about it, whether it is a spring flower in the middle of a winter-scorched field or a ray of sunshine to brighten an overcast day. Imperfect, yes. But still able to bring us joy. It is a joy that the Creator might not feel Himself as He compares them to what He *wanted* for us. But through our appreciation of them He can enjoy them as well. The same way I enjoy bugs and slugs and creepy, slinky, slimy things. And yes, even grasshoppers.

Chapter 16

FROM THE MOUTHS OF BABES

FROM THE LIPS OF CHILDREN AND INFANTS you have or-dained praise because of your enemies, to silence the foe and the avenger. Psalm 8:2.

I know I didn't move it.

I remembered sorting the mail while I watched the kids take their bath. I laid down the pile I wanted to keep, including a large royalty check from one of my publishers, on the bathroom counter. And I know I didn't move it, because every time I thought about where that pile of mail was my brain went *zip!* right to the bathroom counter. And I practically have a photographic memory about that sort of thing.

The only problem was that the pile of mail wasn't there. I looked everywhere else, and it wasn't there, either. My frustration rose faster than the space shuttle, and I became more desperate as time passed. I even called my husband at work and asked him where he moved it to, because I was *sure* it hadn't been I. *I* would have remembered. *He* was slightly less than famous for misplacing things.

He said he didn't know where it was, either. I dropped into my desk chair, frustrated, beat, and very angry. I had reached a dead end. I had no idea what to do.

"Mommy, you're never gonna find the mail," Josh told me with typical 5-year-old confidence. I tended to agree with him at the moment.

"Oh yeah? Why's that?"

"'Cause you didn't ask Jesus to help you."

Ouch.

I sighed. "You're right, Josh. I didn't. Will you pray with me now?"

"I already prayed, Mom."

Yikes! Ouch!

You know that stuff that collects in the drain and makes you wrinkle your nose and say *"Eeeew"*? I felt like the stuff that makes *that* stuff say *"Eeeew."*

The Bible says "and a little child shall lead them." Sometimes I think they'll have to because as adults we spend so much time pretending to *be* God that we don't have time to listen to Him.

I suspect that David knew how I felt that day. When he received a visit from Nathan, God's prophet, a lesson from God was probably the last thing on his mind. And, really, it does often seem that we learn the best lessons when we aren't particularly looking for them.

"I have a story to tell you," Nathan began, and David settled down eagerly, anticipating high entertainment. A story. Oh, goody!

"In a particular town there lived two men. One was rich and one was poor. The rich man had loads of sheep and cattle, more, really, than he knew what to do with. The poor man had only one, a little ewe lamb that he had bought. He'd raised it, and it grew up with him and his children. It shared his food, drank from his cup, and even slept in his arms. It was like a daughter to him."

"How sweet," David murmured, leaning forward on the edge of his seat, trying to guess the ending.

"Now, a traveler hitchhiked into town one day and went to stay with the rich man. Knowing that he would have to feed the guest, the rich man realized he had a dilemma on his hands. He didn't want to butcher one of his own sheep or cows for the traveler. Then it came to him! An epiphany! He took the *poor man's* sheep and prepared it for the traveler to eat, so he could spare his own flocks and herds."

"He *what?*" David roared, bolting out of his chair. His face turned purple and the veins in his neck bulged. "What a cad! Whoever he is, he deserves to die! He must pay four times over for that lamb, that's all there is to it. Only a complete reprobate would do such a thing and not even feel sorry for it."

David had no idea there was a lesson coming. Nathan looked David square in the eye and said, "You are the man."

Yikes! Ouch!

All David's hot air dissipated. Suddenly he felt very cold. Everyone around him melted into the back of his consciousness. The words "You are the man" were ringing in his ears. The lesson embedded itself. Images coursed through his mind, flashes, bursts of understanding.

There was Bathsheba, his lovely Bathsheba, Uriah's lovely Bathsheba, bathing on the rooftop. And he saw his orders purposely placing Uriah where he would be killed in battle. Uriah died attempting to protect Israel and David, who had stolen his wife. David saw his wedding to Bathsheba—how happy they were. And through it all he saw his own hand leading the way, not God's.

Sweat trickled down his back, and his palms felt hot and itchy. He slowly came back to the present. Nathan was there, a very tangible reminder of what had transpired. David sank back onto his throne. His mouth was dry. His heart was pounding. He had learned a very difficult lesson.

"I already prayed, Mom."

It's impossible to express the clarity of mind you experience at such a moment. Only if you have been there do you recognize the feeling. It's as if a vacuum is created into which everything except this one lesson is sucked. The rest of your life ceases to exist for a single instant while you process this burst of insight.

The most overwhelming feelings at such a time are humility and awe. It's impossible to mistake a message like this. You know with absolute certainty that God has paused and is present in this moment. And what's more, He has a message for you. Specifically for you. No one else. It's your message. Is that awesome, or what?

In my case, that He used my 5-year-old child to tell me something so important was particularly painful. And effective. Here is a small being who relies on me for everything. I provide him with food. I provide him with comfort. I nurture him. I instill values in him. About the only thing I don't do is look to him to teach me a lesson about faith.

And that is probably why it was so effective.

It has certainly stuck with me. Not that I don't forget it at times. I still like to think I know it all. It's hard for me to give up control long enough to let God take over. I have a strong tendency to run the show. This quality of my personality makes me successful in my career, but it can really get in the way of an intimate relationship with God, because we can't both be in control. Someone has to be the ultimate authority. And too often I rely on myself to fill that position.

"I already prayed, Mom."
And a little child shall lead them.
Who's in control of your life today?

I CALL HIM ABBA

Chapter 17

DISCIPLINE

THOSE WHOM I LOVE I rebuke and discipline. So be earnest, and repent. Revelation 3:19.

I'll never forget the first time I had to discipline Joshua. He was about 9 months old and unbelievably aware. He knew early what yes and no meant. I was giving him a bath in the kitchen sink when he reached out and knocked a plant on the windowsill into the water I was bathing him in. I said "No" firmly and put the plant back. He gave me a wicked little look and did it again.

I repeated, "No," and put it back. The third time I decided I needed something to back up my words. I put his chubby little hand in the palm of mine and spanked it, hitting my own hand more than his. I felt horrible. I was nearly in tears. It didn't bother Joshua at all.

He grinned and did it again.

And again.

And again.

This went on for at least 15 minutes. Every time I spanked his hand I felt worse and longed for the ordeal of correction to be over. I was severely tempted to simply stop. By the tenth time, I was ready to give up and say, "Who cares about an old flowerpot, anyway? It's not such a big deal."

My reaction to discipline had nothing to do with how Josh felt about it. He continued to reach for the flowerpot, unfazed. My attempts to distract him or correct him were futile at best and merely annoying at worst. And as much as it pained me I continued doggedly with my efforts until he finally left the flowerpot alone. In the end I felt like the one who had been sorely used.

Since that day at the beginning of my career in discipline, I've discovered much more creative ways to discipline my children. I've learned the benefit of distraction and alternate activities. But I've also found that the cardinal rule of discipline is: consistency. I've also learned that consistency is very difficult.

Because to be consistent you really have to be dedicated to making a difference. No one likes to see another human being go through a difficult time, and when that human being is your child, someone you bore, nursed, and snuggled, it's almost impossible. Unless you have a bigger picture in mind. You don't see the correction in light of the moment; you see it in terms of what it will ultimately accomplish in the life of your child. And that's really the only way it is possible.

The other problem with consistency is that it's easy to get tired and relax your standards.

Joshua was playing with clay one afternoon. When he got bored he thought he would just move on to something else. As he hopped down from the table I caught the mess of clay out of the corner of my eye.

"Josh, I want you to pick up the clay before you do something else."

He gave me an appraising look, as if trying to decide just how serious I was. "No, I don't want to."

"Yes, honey, you need to pick up the clay. I don't want a mess on the table."

He switched smoothly into whining gear. "But I don't want to. I can't do it myself. You have to help me."

"I'll hold the bag," I agreed. "You put the clay inside."

"No, I don't want to. I can't. It's too hard."

"Joshua, you're not leaving the table until you put the clay in the bag."

One movement was all it would take. All he had to do was lift the lump of clay and place it in the bag. Instead, he sat and pouted. Occasionally he broke into a whine about how unfair his circumstance was. At times he begged to be allowed to get down from the table.

For three interminable hours I longed to tell him to go ahead. One word from me, a simple "OK," would release him from all his trouble. But what would that teach him? That rules were made to be broken.

Except we know they're not.

But, oh, can they be hard to uphold!

The whisper of Lucifer's rebellion spread like wildfire. God choked back a gut-wrenching feeling in the pit of His stomach. Heaven's peace was rifled with conflict. It had started. He sighed, His breath catching. From this moment on He would have to maintain discipline. And, oh, how hard it would be! How weary He would get. Time stretched in front of Him.

No parent wants to discipline. It's so much easier to let things slide, to overlook transgressions. It's tempting to ask why God didn't just brush sin under the celestial carpet when it first erupted. Why did He make such a big deal out of it? Why not just let bygones be bygones and give the transgressors another chance?

"Oh, all right, I know you didn't really mean it. We'll just forget this ever happened. Say no more about it."

Wouldn't that have solved everything? Lucifer could take his place back with the angels. The fallen angels would resume their places as well. Life would go on exactly as they all knew it. Nothing would be different. There would be no pain as a consequence to this choice of Lucifer's to believe himself equal with God and try to undermine God's authority.

We aren't privileged to know the full consequences that judging Lucifer's act of rebellion with such shortsightedness would have caused. But we can speculate. Because sin, once it took hold in Lucifer's heart, would not have let go so easily. Like cancer, it would have continued to corrode his heart. Possibly additional angels would have been lost if it had been allowed to continue in heaven.

You see, ignoring wrong is selfish. It indulges us and our distaste for pain. It's the easy way out. No matter how He longed to ignore sin, God couldn't take the easy way out because He loves us too much. And if we love our children we won't take the easy way out either.

Discipline is hard. Yes, it is hard. But when discipline is accepted and you see contrition and growth as a result of your efforts, it is worthwhile. When you hold a child who has just been corrected, and see genuine repentance and understanding of sin's effects, you know that all the pain of standing your ground is worthwhile.

All children will grow up and ultimately make their own decisions about life and God. But if they start out with the best base possible in the form of loving discipline, they will be much better equipped to maintain their balance on the straight and narrow road to heaven's eternal rewards. When I get tired and feel like giving up, I can remember that God never gives up on me.

And really, isn't that what it's all about in the first place?

Chapter 18

THE GOOD, THE BAD, AND THE UGLY

SHALL WE ACCEPT GOOD FROM GOD, and not trouble? Job 2:10.

I loved him. I did. There was no question about that. Even if he had kept me up 24 hours a day, screaming at the top of his lungs, looking at Joshua's sweet face and cuddling his tiny body would have made me forget all manner of abuse against my sanity in the form of sleep deprivation and noise pollution.

I had waited an awful long time to have a child of my own.

And I overlooked a lot. He was a colicky baby and had trouble going to sleep, staying asleep, and waking up. There was virtually no time of the day when he didn't have to be entertained, soothed, or have some need met. Simple tasks such as dressing him resembled a roadshow. I had to sing, tickle, and distract him or he would start squirming and wailing. Mothering turned into a very tiring profession. I felt as though I was straining to please him but that I never measured up.

Still, I loved it and I wouldn't have traded motherhood for anything in the world. Despite his contrariness, Joshua was a possessive baby. He clung to me in a very gratifying manner whenever he was around strangers, or even friends and family for that matter, or whenever I went away, whether just into the next room or for a short, infrequent excursion out of the house. "I waited so long for a child," I would cry on Rob's shoulder. "Why did God send me a difficult baby?"

I considered Joshua's conception nothing short of a miracle, since it happened about the time I had given up hope of ever becoming pregnant; I never really expected to have more children. Besides, I wasn't sure I could *handle* another child. After all, no matter how hard I tried, I wasn't doing such a great job of keeping Josh happy. How could I possibly fulfill the needs of two children?

But when Rachel arrived I had a sweet surprise.

"God knew what He was doing," I told Rob confidently. He had given me a difficult child first when I was so desperate for a child that my patience was at an all-time high. Then, when I was worn down, He sent me a gentle, easy-tempered baby girl, who seemed to go out of her way to please me.

Except for one thing.

Where Joshua had been difficult and clingy, Rachel was mild-mannered and aloof. She didn't particularly care for nursing, though she nursed. It was more of a survival instinct than a comfort mechanism, as it had been for Joshua. To my horror I realized that *she didn't particularly need me.*

Well, I mean, she needed me to change her and feed her and protect her from sharp objects, but she didn't need me emotionally, like Joshua had. Early on, she demonstrated an independent streak. It was heartbreaking. I wanted to cuddle her, tickle her toes, blow raspberries on her tummy, but she was more interested in whatever else was going on.

I felt rejected.

THE GOOD, THE BAD, AND THE UGLY

And I wondered if that isn't maybe how God feels when I get caught up in my own independence. When Martha and I start looking like twins.

"Martha?"

"Yeah?"

"Whacha doin'?"

"Oh, you wouldn't believe I've got to get all the food ready for the party tonight. There's going to be a horde here, and I've already been up all night. I'm sure I'm going to run out of something. If I could figure out what it was, I'd stock up right now. I'm so tired I don't even know what I'm doing exactly. I feel like I'm running around chasing my tail."

"Martha?"

"Just a minute. If I don't do something with this dough it's going to flop and then where will I be? Without bread. Can you imagine anything so embarrassing? As soon as I do this I can take care of sweeping the floor. Oh, and stoking the fire. And I forgot, I have to boil some water. Where is Mary? Why have I got to do all this by myself? It's a good thing I've got such control of the situation. Still, I wish I had a *little* help."

"Martha?"

"What?"

"You sound tired and you're getting irritable."

"Well, I know that. You think I don't know that? I'm exhausted, that's what I am. I passed tired ages ago. And look at my hair! All this fussing in the kitchen made it so limp and it's fallen into my eyes. I'll have to fix it back up again. I can't believe it! I just spilled stew on my skirt. Now I'm going to have to change into something else before I can serve the guests.

"Where *is* that Mary? Just wait until I get my hands on her. Leaving me to do all the work. The ungrateful little wretch. What can she be doing? Ouch! There, that does it, now I've burned my hand. I'll have to go get some aloe. Where is *Mary?*"

"Here I am, Martha. I'm listening to the Master."

"What? Just sitting there while I work myself to death? Lord, aren't You going to do something about this? Oh, great, now on top of everything else I'm going to cry!"

"Martha?"

"WHAT IS IT, LORD?"

"Martha, don't you *need* Me?"

"Why, no, Lord, I don't think so."

We can be independent. We can be self-sufficient. We can be in control. But at some point we are going to need someone. And it's often at the most inconvenient times, too. After all, it's not so bad to need someone when you're still feeling slightly in control of the situation. Then you can manipulate just how much help you have to receive and dictate precisely how you want to receive it.

The problem is that by the time we *really* need someone we are usually in such bad shape that we don't have any say in the situation. It's like being force-fed. If you aren't used to eating from someone else's hand in the first place you could choke to death. When we have this trouble in accepting help or good things from others or from God, imagine what happens when we need to accept bad things. How much harder that makes it for us to learn, grow, and be graceful as we move through life.

The Bible says pride goes before destruction. Think how much better off we'd be if pride would just go, period. The same God who put Psalms after Job in the Bible gives us good times and bad times, easy children and difficult children. And it shouldn't be so much a question of why as it should be a prayer of thanks! Our battle cry would change from *resist!* to *Thy will be done!* and we would discover that there is an eternity of difference between the two.

THE GOOD, THE BAD, AND THE UGLY

If I could just drop the act and admit I don't know it all, it would be easier for me to cuddle up to God's chest and accept whatever came from His hand as in my best interest. And it'll come. Every time Rachel puts her chubby arms around my neck, pats my back, and lays her curly blond head on my shoulder, filling me with gratitude for her sweetness, I'm confident that it'll come. The best things in life often take time.

Chapter 19

JUMPING IN
WITH BOTH FEET

FOR THE LORD TAKES DELIGHT in his people; he crowns the humble with salvation. Psalm 149:4.

"Mom, will you play Animals, Animals Talk with me?"

The 15 free minutes stretching invitingly before me melted into oblivion when I heard the request. The dreaded Animals, Animals Talk was Josh's favorite game, in which his many animals simply talked to each other. Of course, being the grown-up, I usually had to do all the "talking" while he just moved his animals around and thought up scenarios for them to enact. Rob was really much better at it than I was, creating such things as imaginary beings named Grickles, and developing mysteries for the animals to solve.

I sighed. "Yeah, I guess so."

While he assembled the animals, choosing some for himself and some for me, I fidgeted, ruing the forfeiture of my free time. I made up silly voices for my animals, but my mind was on what I would be doing when the tedious game was over. I didn't put anything special into the game. I merely went through the motions of play. Maybe Josh couldn't tell, but I could.

Because I could remember what it was like when playing was my life. I couldn't even imagine growing up and getting a job and having responsibilities and not being able to play. My imagination ran as wild as the things I made up to do and I never had a lack of playmates.

The last time I remembered really losing myself in play was on my eighteenth birthday. My youngest sister, Joy, was 6 years old. I spent the entire morning playing with her in the dirt outside on the driveway. We made sand cakes and played marbles. I felt utterly carefree. Even the problems and insecurities of being 18 and facing an unknown future faded away for awhile. It made me feel like a kid again. I was so impressed that I wrote about it in my journal, freezing the moment in time.

When I had my own kids I was too busy being mom to play with them much. In fact, playing was a hard thing for me to do. I forced myself, sure, because kids need their parents to play with them. But I didn't often enjoy it.

Occasionally, though, I would have a day or an hour when playing was fun. The incredible responsibilities attached to being a grown-up melted away, and I could enjoy being a kid with my kids. Digging in the sandpile, I was once again 6, making dirt cakes with my next-door neighbor, Robin, who used to shock her mother by eating the sand. Playing a game of lawn tennis, I would forget for a little while that I wasn't playing with my buddies on the front lawn, hoping that dinner would be late so I could play longer. Throwing the baseball for Josh, I concentrated more on his swing than on my agenda.

There were moments, glimpses that reminded me there was more to playing than what I was getting out of it all the time. That there was more to having children than just taking care of

I CALL HIM ABBA

them. There could also be fun and enjoyment. And delight. I could delight in my children the way God delighted in me.

Because God didn't just create man. He also spent time enjoying him. We know they walked together in the garden, but I like to imagine they did other things too. Perhaps they twirled around as fast as they could until they got dizzy, then fell laughing onto their backs on the soft grass, picking out pictures in the clouds as the sky swirled around. Maybe they plucked wide blades of grass and held them—just so—between their thumbs and blew, making a piercing whistle that drew the curious stares of all the animals. They might even have played animal charades, taking turns acting out the different animals and guessing.

I can't think of anything God created that didn't fall under the category of delightful. Everything He made delighted Him. And unlike us, He let nothing stand in the way of enjoying the delight that His creations provided. "I was filled with delight day after day, rejoicing always in his presence, rejoicing in his whole world and delighting in mankind" (Prov. 8:30, 31).

A friend of mine told me recently (now, bear in mind, this is a 43-year-old man), "Céleste, do you know what I've been doing lately? Jumping in puddles. And you know what? It's *fun!* You know, I never did that as a kid. Now, I'm jumping in with both feet."

Jumping in with both feet. Total abandon. Enjoying the moment. Making every second count. Delight. I want these words to apply to the time I spend playing with my kids. Not only for their sakes—though they will undoubtedly receive a great benefit from it—but for my sake as well. God the Father didn't meet Adam and Eve in the garden each evening, anxiously monitoring His wristwatch, hoping to get through their time together as quickly as possible. He didn't meet Adam and Eve for their benefit alone. He enjoyed their time together as well.

And I don't think it's possible to enjoy anyone's company, your children's, your spouse's, your friend's, or even God's, without first giving yourself permission to do it. Because otherwise we come loaded with baggage—deadlines, appointments, to-do lists, obligations, distractions. When God met with Adam and Eve it isn't likely His mind was on the next galaxy He planned to create, or an upcoming meeting with the cherubim.

We have to put our concerns on hold and allow ourselves to live in *this* moment and not the next 30.

So much of what we burden ourselves with is unnecessary. Sure, some is unavoidable if we are functioning people in a fast-paced world. But if we can teach ourselves to lay it aside for a little while, we will discover an aspect of life that we sorely lack—delight.

And in the discovery, maybe we will see that the most basic, most primary need of our hearts is relationships. Close, intimate relationships with the people that we cherish. Because nothing lasts forever, and delight is something that should be grabbed with two-fisted resolve, whenever the opportunity presents itself.

You might see it in a garden, on the lawn, at the park, in the library, on the phone, or in the living room. Wherever you come across an opportunity to experience delight, seize it and savor it. Before it slips away.

ALMOST CHILDREN

BEFORE I FORMED YOU IN THE WOMB I knew you, before you were born I set you apart. Jeremiah 1:5.

One day I woke up and they were just there. Everywhere, as if they had always existed and I had never noticed. There were crowds of them on the playground, playing hide and seek behind their mothers, who stood talking. I call them the "almost children" because they are almost there.

The other children are solid and bright, but the "almost children" are transparent. If you concentrate hard enough you can see right through them. Their happy voices, shrieking with laughter as they play, sound far away, like faded joy. Their parents seem oblivious to them for the most part, except for a few here and there staring, intent, seeming as if they can almost hear the far-off childish giggles and see the smiling upturned faces begging to be noticed.

Why are they here, these "almost children"? Why are there so many? Four or five group around some of the mothers.

Sometimes even more. How could they not notice them? Have they ever noticed them? I can see them clearly as day.

I break away from my mother's side to run with them and play. That's when I notice that if I concentrate hard enough I can see right through my hand.

I look up at my mother. She stares through me, thinking, not seeing me.

"Why?" I ask, but there is no answer. "Didn't you love me?" I cry.

Her silence mocks me. "God gave you a miracle," I tell her. "A miracle just for you."

She doesn't answer me. A long, mournful sigh whistles through her lips. Then she turns to walk away, and I am left to join the "almost children."

When I found out I was pregnant I wanted the world to know. I couldn't wait to tell everyone. It was months before I would "show," and I was bursting to share my fantastic news. So I told everyone I knew.

One well-intentioned woman took me aside. "Dear, you shouldn't really say anything—you know, about your condition—just yet."

I stared at her blankly. "Why not?"

She cleared her throat and glanced politely down at the floor. "Well, you know, what if you lose the baby?"

I was still blank. "Yes? What if I lose the baby?"

She was obviously embarrassed—for *me*. "Why, then you'd have to tell everyone, and it would be just awful."

"Yes," I assured her, finally having caught her drift. "Yes, if I lost my baby it would be awful. And I would have a funeral and I would expect everyone I know to be there. Because this baby is a person and is real to me already."

I CALL HIM ABBA

The unbelievably priceless gift of life—new life—sharpened my focus. Shortly after Joshua was born I remember being near a woman I knew who had had several abortions. She was holding her new baby, and suddenly I had the distinct impression that became the basis for the opening illustration in this chapter. For an instant those children were so clear to me that I could have reached out and touched them.

I saw them wonder why she had given them up but had chosen to keep the child in her arms. The hurt in their eyes was overwhelming. In it I saw the reflections of millions of God's children who had been "aborted." By choosing not to follow Him they had become like the "almost children."

We've all seen pictures of Earth taken from space. From the porthole window of a spaceship our globe is reduced to a silent, spinning orb of swirling blue and white. Seen in the context of space, with the backdrop of our universe, Planet Earth seems particularly insignificant, inspiring awe in more than one astronaut. From their vantage point our world is reduced to a rubber-bouncy ball with a pretty pattern.

Frank Borman was commander of the first space crew to travel beyond the earth's orbit. Looking down on the earth from 250,000 miles away, Borman radioed back a message, quoting Genesis 1:1: "In the beginning, God created the heavens and the earth" (KJV). As he later explained, "I had an enormous feeling that there had to be a power greater than any of us— that there was a God, that there was indeed a beginning."

When we look at Earth in relation to the galaxy and other universes and spaces beyond even our most advanced capabilities to penetrate, we become even more puny in our own estimation. It staggers the mind that God, seeing Earth as even smaller than our cameras have been able to show it to us, looks down at it and cares so strongly *for each one of us.*

Earth spins upon its axis slowly, compared to the speed at which our brains spin, caught in the frantic pace of life as it races past us. We careen with abandon from one project to the next, one love to the next, one job to the next. Stability isn't a part of our lives any longer. People move and sever relationships, leaving us without support systems. We are more materially comfortable than ever before and in most cases more unhappy than ever before.

Clinging to this grassy slope, we are happy if we can only hang on—never mind about accomplishing great things. Let's just keep the dog in Kibbles and be sure we get the kids to their umpteen appointments. Dashing around at the speed of light, we neglect the very relationship that is the most important. You know what I'm talking about. You do it. I do it, too. There are just so many other things that come first.

Even *good* things should not be put above God. He has to be first or everything else we do will be last. I don't want to be one of the "almost children." I don't want to be one of His children who aren't really there. I don't want to be one of the ones He sighs for and longs to hold in His arms.

I want to feel solid against His chest, like my children feel solid when I hold them. I don't want to be just a regret, a lost opportunity. I want to be the daughter who pesters Him to tell stories and play games and go for walks. I want to see the twinkle in His eye when I (elaborately) relate an outing we took. I want to draw pictures that He will hang on the walls, even if the people have arms sticking out of their ears and their noses look like pig snouts.

I may annoy Him at times. I may cause Him to choke on laughter. I may even exasperate Him. But I want to be *there*. I don't want to be an "almost child." I don't want my laughter to sound hollow and His eyes to mist over when He thinks about me. We can trick ourselves into thinking that we're going along OK, we're managing. But the truth is that we are either one or the other. We're God's child or we're "almost children."

"I know your deeds," God says, "that you are neither cold nor hot. I wish you were either one or the other! So, because you are lukewarm—neither hot nor cold—I am about to spit you out of my mouth" (Rev. 3:15, 16).

Strong words? Yes. Strong Father? Yes.

And because He is so strong, He can pull us out of ourselves and our preoccupation with our own circles of problems. He can lead us to the fountain of water, but only we can drink out of it. Take long draughts. That water will make you strong, and no one, absolutely no one, will ever be able to see through you.

Chapter 21

GOD WITH US

NOW THE DWELLING OF GOD IS WITH MEN, and he will live with them. They will be his people, and God himself will be with them and be their God. Revelation 21:3.

The sparkle had nothing to do with the tiny lights twinkling in the darkness from hundreds of homes lit up for the season. It was in Joshua's eyes as he told me what he was looking forward to during the Christmas season. He was charged with excitement. I could almost hear the crackle of static electricity as he talked.

"Christmas is my most bestest time of the year," he informed me. "I like opening my stocking on Christmas morning. And I like the cookies we make. Those little kinds that we put frosting on." His fingers wiggled descriptively for my benefit.

"Sugar cookies," I supplied.

"I like it when we go get the Christmas tree," he went on. "We have hot cider, and you get a new ornament for the tree.

I'm going to put candy canes and cookies on the tree this year. Can we do that?"

"You mean those gingerbread cookies we hang from the tree? Sure. You know, when you were little you used to call those Nummies."

"I did?" He seemed pleased that he had coined such an interesting word. "And I like getting presents, but it's even better than my birthday because on my birthday I don't get a stocking. Do you think my stuffed bear could have a stocking too?"

"We'll see. I suppose so. I'm going to make us all new stockings this year, so I'll make little ones for you and Rachel to use for your favorite stuffed animals. How does that sound?"

Watching him get so excited over Christmas made me remember all the things that had made Christmas special for me as a child. My mother always played Christmas music a couple weeks before Christmas. She played the same records every year and finally I was beginning to recognize them. Andy Griffith. Burl Ives. Bing Crosby.

I can remember one December day. It might have been for me, like Joshua, the first time I really knew what was coming. The first time I could anticipate Christmas. "Have a holly jolly Christmas, it's the best time of the year," crooned Burl Ives as I stared out the window at the softly falling snow. It wasn't hard to imagine that Christmas would live up to its reputation.

I believed him. I had faith that yes, this *would* be the best time of the year. Great smells permeated the kitchen where my mother baked toothsome treats in preparation for the holiday. There were rustlings and whispering as Christmas secrets were formulated and carried out. The music on the record player (Eeks! Vinyl!) brought back vague, pleasant memories. Yes, Christmas *must* be the best time of the year.

And truly we do seem to put aside the ugliness of life as

GOD WITH US   97 much as possible during the Christmas season. It's as if, even if we don't always capture the true meaning of Christmas, we can *sense* what it is . . . or what it was. We can feel how it all started.

The first Christmas was lit by only one light. A bright point in the heavens, surely, but only one. Nothing for the electric companies to get excited about. Yet that one star pinpointed the most glorious spot on all of earth where the dwelling of God was with men. Which is, of course, what Christmas is all about.

We often fail to see the meaning, buried as we are in ribbons, packages, and bows. The volume of Christmas carols often stills the whisper of truth they strive to proclaim. We've sung them so many times the words hardly sink in anymore. The day after Christmas we toss out the tree, burn the crumpled wrapping paper, and forget about peace on earth for another year. Unless God is truly *with* us we might just as well.

But it doesn't have to be that way, because the miracle of Christmas is alive every day of the year.

Emmanuel. God *with* us.

Say it out loud.

Say it again. Like you mean it.

God with us!

That is the miracle of Christmas. God came to our planet and walked our dusty roads and ate our food. He was with us. He dwelt with us. He counseled us. He comforted us. That is what we are celebrating. You do not get extra points for buying gifts you can't afford, or for purchasing presents for people you barely tolerate. There is no bonus credit if your Christmas card list goes over the 100 mark or you are awarded five star status for your decorating skills. It's not about indulgence—it's about surrender.

Before God can move in and be with us we've got to free up some space. He won't elbow His way in and wedge Himself in a corner of our hearts. He wants the place all to Himself; He doesn't need any roommate of questionable character. Because even roommates you trust can turn out to be deadbeats.

When my sister Joy was going to college in Tennessee she rented an apartment. Classes let out in the spring and she decided to go home for the summer, so she allowed a friend of hers to use her apartment while she was gone. She returned to find that not only had the roommate invited her boyfriend to live with her (in my sister's bed!) but he had been using her car and ruined it.

God won't force His way into your heart today any more than He would have forced His way into the inn, but meekly accepted birth in a dirty stable. It has to be your choice, your decision. Because He wants to be your guest.

Mary groans with each labor pain. Her hands grip the sides of her extended abdomen. They grope and knead the taut flesh. She wishes she could just push the baby out. But all things take time. All the best things take time. There are hours as she squats over the clean straw when she doesn't think she's going to make it, after all. Her heart will break before her baby is born.

Now imagine another birth. This one has taken thousands of years to gestate. Heaven is pregnant, ready to burst. Labor pains grip all its inhabitants. They wish they could speed things up, but their hands are tied. They can do nothing but wait and watch. And sometimes they feel as though their hearts will break before this baby is born, and God is once again, literally, with us.

One Christmas leads to another in a parade of anticipation. Memories of Christmases past heighten our expectations. Jesus' birth in the stable, my Christmas as a child, Joshua's Christmas memories, and soon Rachel's, all serve to bring us one step closer to the ultimate Christmas experience. When Jesus will throw open the gates of heaven and invite us inside. And we will live with God forever. We will be His people and He will be our God.

God will be *with* us.

Emmanuel!

Chapter 22

DISTRACTIONS

NOW CHOOSE LIFE, so that you and your children may live and that you may love the Lord your God, listen to his voice, and hold fast to him. For the Lord is your life, and he will give you many years in the land he swore to give to your fathers, Abraham, Isaac and Jacob. Deuteronomy 30:19, 20.

There are summer days that pull you outside with their intensity. It is simply impossible to resist the bright sun. The rustling leaves. The blue sky. The warm grass under your bare feet. On those days I chuck responsibilities such as house-cleaning and weed-pulling for the soft sand and almost unbearable cold water of our favorite rec center.

The picnic basket is packed with sandwiches, cold water bottles, fruit, snacks, and a paperback I will not have a chance to read. We bring wet facecloths sensibly packed in plastic baggies, towels, an old quilt to spread on the beach, and the strongest sunblock known to man. Joshua and Rachel load their plastic sand buckets with beach toys, peel on their swimsuits, and they're ready to go. I do a quick change into my favorite sun-dress, flip-flops, and sunglasses. Our house cannot contain us.

These outings always seem simpler in theory than they are in practice. In theory we get to the beach, lay out our blanket (neatly), eat our lunch, and then the children play in the sand and splash in the water while I recline on my blanket and do some reading. In practice we stagger out to the beach, loaded down with picnic gear; the children are too excited to eat and what they do attempt to consume ends up smeared on the quilt. Then, because they are rather shy, they tug on my dress and whine that I should go down to the water with them or help them build something in the sand 'cause a *kid* is there and *kids* can be scary people. So I tramp down to the water, get my dress wet, and I never do get to read more than the title of the book I brought.

Occasionally, Josh will make a pint-sized friend or get in-terested in the other side of the beach (where the frogs are). He will gradually get bolder, sometimes crossing the sand without me, walking in front of kids who are swinging, or wading so far into the water that it actually becomes dangerous because if he falls he can't swim. At those times I do what a normal, panic-stricken mother would do. I scream at the top of my lungs and get hysterical.

You would think that the sight of me would stop any kid (or adult for that matter) dead in their tracks, but usually at this point Joshua is so interested in what he's doing that I have be-come inconsequential. He's so distracted that he doesn't even notice me. I could drop dead on the sand and he wouldn't even be aware of it.

"Stop! Wait! Come back!" It's almost like shrieking in a vac-uum. Nothing happens. He's oblivious. I tear across the sand or into the water, running in slow motion. I grab him, breathless.

"Where are you going? What are you doing? Be careful! You nearly walked into that kid who was swinging."

With the pressure of my hands grasping his arms I see realization spread in his eyes. Earth to Josh! He comes slowly back to reality and considers the danger he was in. "It's OK. I wasn't watching where I was going. I'll be all right now. Don't worry."

When I first became a parent the scariest revelation of it was the responsibility. You are responsible for a *life*. You hold life in the palm of your hand—literally. If you mess up, that life is snuffed out. If you relax your vigil, it will be gone with swiftness so sudden that it will take your breath away forever. When you are a card-carrying control freak like I am, this hits you very hard.

It's what makes parents so protective. It's what makes us tiptoe into our children's room every night to make sure they are covered up and breathing, and that the room isn't too hot or too cold. It's what makes us leery of baby-sitters and turns us into voracious readers who can consume entire baby reference books in a single sitting.

It's a little easier to watch children who aren't mobile, but once they start scooting around, look out. They are apt to end up anywhere. Not always is it the result of down-and-out disobedience. Sometimes they just stop paying attention to the warning signs and forget where they are.

Israel was constantly compromising herself this way. So much so that she nearly drove God her Father to distraction. "All day long I have held out my hands to an obstinate people, who walk in ways not good, pursuing their own imaginations" (Isa. 65:2). Her imagination led her hither and yon, following one pipe dream after another.

God tried everything. He sent prophets to give warning messages. He tried pillars of cloud and fire. He parted seas and provided armies of angels. He made a donkey talk and deaf men hear. He made the lame to dance and the guilty innocent. And when all else failed, He died for them. And even that wasn't enough to get their attention.

He stood on the beach hopping up and down waving His arms and whistling, but nothing happened. They didn't even turn around to see what all the commotion was about. They weren't tuned in, so they didn't catch the warnings.

They were too distracted by everything else that was going on around them. It's easy to get distracted. The danger lies in the fact that it's hard to figure out you are distracted. It usually hits you on the blind side. Not something you expected to do. Not always deliberate.

You hear the faint warning bells, the unease that maybe you are venturing where you ought not to go. You might see swinging legs brush through the air past your arm, or feel the water rise to a higher level on your chest than you have ever felt before. And there might be a queasy feeling in the pit of your stomach. These warning signs, if ignored, will lead to your demise. Before you realize it, you will be in trouble.

It's hard to say what will distract someone because it's different for every person. With Josh, those frogs were a strong enticement. They were so interesting that, for the time being, everything else was forgotten. He even put aside his fear of being separated from me in order to pursue his interest in the frogs. He *wanted* one of those frogs.

For me, it's not frogs. For you either, I bet. But there is something, some thing, that will attract you so strongly that you will block out all warning signs, deafen your ears to any shouts of warning, and blind your eyes to everything around you except that one thing.

But you can stay focused.

Interested?

It comes down to one solitary strategy.

If Josh had come to me first about leaving to look at frogs, or asked me what I thought about going farther into the water, I would have guided him or accompanied him. If he had accepted my help to do the things he was interested in doing, he could have done them safely. And if what he wanted to do wasn't in his best interest I could have told him that and steered him in an appropriate direction.

Draw any parallels there? Yeah, me too. I know I have trouble seeing God as a constant companion, stuck to my hip, as it were. I prefer to see Him as a celestial compass, kept in my pocket until needed. I could take a reading now and then. The rest of the time I would be free to meander in whichever direction took my fancy.

But it doesn't work that way any more than it does for Joshua and me. He and I have to stay in constant contact in order for me to provide him constant guidance. I realize that as Joshua gets older he will require less and less guidance from me. And that's natural for him or any child. Paradoxically, as I get older I will require more and more guidance from God. Because it will become clearer that only when I am truly surrendered to Him and leaning on Him can I reach my fullest potential.

When that happens I won't have any blind sides because He will be watching all of them for me.

Chapter 23

WALKING HEARTS

SO GOD CREATED MAN IN HIS OWN IMAGE, in the image of God he created him; male and female he created them. Genesis 1:27.

I've always been afraid of heights. There was the time I climbed out onto a rock gangplank on the way up Mount Mansfield, and froze. Someone had to come out and pull me back, because I took one look down and my limbs became paralyzed. I couldn't do anything more than cling to the rough surface and be thankful I wasn't alone when I tried such a stunt.

Another time, on a trip to Nova Scotia, Rob and I got caught on a beach when the tide came in. The lighthouse operator had told us that it came in fast and not to get caught on the rocks. There was only one way up—to climb the rocky face of a cliff to the lighthouse. With the water rushing in higher with each pulsing wave, we didn't have much choice, so up we went.

"Don't look down," Rob repeated, urging me higher and higher on the jagged wall of the cliff. Miraculously, we found a goat path that snaked to the top of the outcropping. I avoided looking down, goaded by fear, until we were at the top.

If my mother had been there either time she would have easily matched my terror with her own. I know this because of one experience. My parents and I had hiked Algonquin Mountain, the second-highest peak in the Adirondacks, with some friends in the winter. On the icy, bald surface of the mountain, just before we reached the top, my instep crampons suddenly slipped and I was tipped onto the toes of my hiking boots on the slippery rocks. I started to slide over the side of the mountain, unable to do anything to help myself.

"Mom! I'm slipping!"

My mother was near the edge by some small brush. I could see barely controlled panic in her eyes. She grabbed a handful of brush and held her other hand out to me. "Grab my hand," she said, stretching as far as she could.

With her pulling me I was able to maneuver back onto my crampons and get some traction to climb to safer ground. If she had not been there I would have been a small, broken speck miles below. Fortunately, I'm here to write about it instead.

When you have a child it's like pulling your heart out of your chest cavity and allowing it to walk around outside your body for the rest of your life. There's no telling what might happen to it. And if that heart is careless, either deliberately or by accident, you pay an enormous price for your vulnerability.

I know all about this. From the first moment Joshua lay in my arms to the last time I rescued one of my children from a catastrophe, I have experienced this vulnerability up close and personal. I really think it has a lot in common with baring your back to the scourge. Let me explain.

Ever since Adam took his first breath, God's heart began to walk around outside His body. It was at the mercy of Adam's will. Whatever Adam decided to do, it hurt or benefited not

WALKING HEARTS

only himself but God as well. You might say that it hurt God worse than it hurt Adam. Because Adam suffered only from the choice. God suffered watching Adam suffer. Besides that, He suffered from the "if onlys":

"If only Adam had listened to My instruction."

"If only Adam had stood strong and resisted temptation."

"If only Adam had stayed within My grasp, I could have caught him."

The "if onlys" are nightmarish because they twist your heart around. There might not have been any if only . . . But, in order for love to thrive, there has to be the possibility of "if onlys." If there isn't, then free choice is gone, and a world without free choice wouldn't be much of a place to live.

There is a saying that goes something like this: "If you love something, set it free. If it comes back to you, it's yours. If it doesn't, it never belonged to you in the first place." It's the letting go, physically and emotionally, that's so hard to do. Because there's no telling what will happen next.

I was in the garden when the most horrible event in my life took place. I was picking herbs to make supper. Life was pretty good. I had no worries. I wasn't thinking about anything in particular. Rob was upstairs with the kids and he ran down through the basement and out the back door for a minute to tell me something.

I remember a fleeting thought about where he might have put Rachel, because I had left her in her walker and she was getting pretty fast in scooting around the house. I might have even asked, because I thought he said she was stuck on the rug in the kitchen.

The next thing I heard curdles my blood to this day.

Kerchunk, kerchunk, kerchunk . . .

I refused to believe it was the sound of walker wheels

rolling down the cellar stairs, even as I raced for the door. When I reached the bottom of the stairs and saw my beautiful baby girl dumped in a heap on the cement floor with the walker on top of her, I went positively hysterical. I remember shaking and hyperventilating and screaming.

I'm not much good in a crisis.

Rachel was fine. She had the tiniest little bump that never even turned black and blue, and a healthy respect for stairs. That was all. But I suffered from a major depression for a week after. All I could think of were the "if onlys."

"If only we hadn't left her alone."

"If only she hadn't been in the walker."

"If only I had been there."

I had flashbacks in which I projected myself into her place. I hurtled down the stairs again and again. Three or four days later, when I barely could still function, my friend Sandy said to me, "Come on, snap out of it. She's OK. She's fine. She's not even hurt. It could have been a *lot* worse. Thank God for protecting her, and move on."

And you're still wondering how I'm going to tie this all in with scourges and bare backs. I'm just coming to that. Hang tight. I know, and maybe you do too, how it feels to have my heart walk, dance, leap, run, skip, and stomp around outside my body. Because that's how God made parenthood. And lest we say that He gives better than He gets, we need look no farther than how we, His children, have treated Him.

When God created Adam, do you suppose He expected one of Adam's children to ply the scourge that whipped the back of His Son into bloody ribbons? Yes, but He created him anyway. And He let Adam go, fully knowing the price it would cost Him. Why? Because He is a parent. He is the fairest, most just parent there ever was or ever will be.

WALKING HEARTS

He knows the cost of letting your heart walk around outside your body. He also knows the sweet rewards. And He wouldn't trade on the value just to spare Himself some pain. Despite the bittersweet agony of it, neither would I.

Chapter 24

KISSING OWIES

FOR THE LAMB AT THE CENTER OF THE THRONE will be their shepherd; he will lead them to springs of living water. And God will wipe away every tear from their eyes. Revelation 7:17.

As a first-time mother I hadn't learned yet what power there is in a mother's kiss. If asked, I would have said the expression "kiss it and make it better" was just that—an expression. But one day I was at my friend Debbie's, and I found out there was a lot more to it than that. Joshua, who was about 2 years old at the time, was playing with Debbie's daughter, Leah, who was a couple months older than he was. I don't remember how it happened, but he hurt himself.

Debbie was closer to him and she helped him up. "Oh, did you get an owie? That's OK, let your Mommy kiss it."

My practical nurse's training could find no medical benefit in kissing an injury, but Debbie had some experience in the area of motherhood, and I was the newcomer. I didn't want to appear stupid, so I said, "Yes, come here, honey, let Mommy kiss it."

I located the boo-boo and kissed it. "There. Is that better?"

To my amazement he said "Yes," and scampered off as if nothing had happened.

I have now kissed hundreds of injuries, from scraped knees to bumped elbows to stubbed toes, and I cannot get over the powerful ability it has to dispel pain. I'm a little surprised that someone hasn't tried to bottle it yet. I mean, a product with that much capacity for relieving pain, restoring security, and providing comfort would easily make someone a millionaire. I can picture the marketing strategy now:

"Mother's Kiss Stick: *Just smear on after injury. Guaranteed to relieve pain. Will not stain."*

"Essence of Kiss de la Mère: *Sprinkle on owie and bask in the warmth of a real mother's love. Repeat as needed."*

"Adhesive Mother's Kisses: *Remove backing and place directly on injury. Mother's kiss will adhere to area and provide instant comfort and pain relief. Contains 100 kisses."*

Consider the potential! It staggers the mind. Imagine a product that can provide instant pain relief—even our sophisticated modern painkillers can't do that. They might be able to temporarily deaden physical pain, but they do nothing for emotional trauma or well-being. They can't make it "all better."

Over the years, kisses have been used for many reasons. From Delilah's seductive smooches to Judas' treacherous peck, kisses can mean one of a hundred things. But the meaning of a mother's kiss has never changed. It continues to have the same result today as it did hundreds of years ago. There is only one other thing in the history of mankind that you can say that about.

The touch of God.

For all we know, he hadn't even wanted to be there. Maybe he muttered the whole time he got dressed and found a torch and accompanied the high priest out of the Temple. He was jostled by others in the crowd and, grumpily, he gave back as good as he got. He was tired. He'd had a long day, and this just wasn't something he was looking forward to.

Not that he had any personal convictions on the matter. But the thought of his warm bed was much more inviting than a waltz through the crowded streets to pick up some braggart. Why couldn't they save things like this for morning, anyway?

He wiped the sleep from his eyes and swallowed a yawn. His irritation increased as he was forced to lengthen his strides to keep up with the high priest, who beckoned angrily for him. "Malchus," the priest growled, "move it, man! Must I carry that torch myself? This is a night for the history books and not fit for sluggards like you. Move, I say!"

And so he had moved, double-stepping as fast as his short legs would carry him, nearly tripping on the high priest's hem as he struggled to keep up. The crowd of soldiers and curiosity seekers poured into the garden like liquid humanity, at once closing off the entrance and surrounding those they came to find. An effective trap if ever there had been one.

Judas, that scoundrel—Malchus had never liked that one—strode up to the man they called Jesus and kissed Him on the cheek. "Greetings, Rabbi!"

Malchus snorted in disgust at the transparency of the man. It was obvious he didn't fool the Teacher, either.

"Friend, do what you came for," Jesus told him.

After that, everything was confusion. Men stepped forward to seize Jesus, and one of His rowdy disciples pulled a sword. Malchus watched it cleave through the night air, illuminated by the light of hundreds of lanterns and torches. It came right for him.

He actually heard the *whoosh* as it cut through the air right by his head. The flat of the blade glanced off his shoulder, but he barely noticed because of the searing pain on the side of his head. His hand, immediately clamping onto his head, felt his ear hanging by a ribbon. Blood oozed from between his fingers. There was a ringing in his head, the shouts of the crowd were dim, although he knew they were louder than anything he had ever heard.

"Your man has maimed my servant," the high priest's voice was shrill and accusing.

"Put your sword back in its place," Jesus said to the man. Malchus could do nothing but look on in shock. "For all who draw the sword will die by the sword."

The next second was one of those he knew he would never forget, no matter how long he lived. Jesus turned to him and pulled his hand away from his ear. He tried to resist, knowing that his ear would come off in his hand. To his amazement, Jesus took his ear—he could even feel His touch. He pressed the ear up against the side of his head where it belonged, and instantly the pain was gone.

When Malchus reached up tentative fingers to explore the area, he found his ear completely intact, exactly where it should be. He was afraid that he had totally lost his hearing for a moment because the crowd in the garden became so quiet. But then he heard a whisper of amazement ripple through the crowd, and he knew that his ear was as good as new.

He walked all the way back to the Temple in awe. He had been touched by God.

Millions have felt that touch. The same touch that restored Malchus' ear has bound up their broken hearts and healed their deep emotional anguish. It has straightened their bent limbs, opened their stopped up ears, and lit their darkened eyes.

I CALL HIM ABBA

Maybe that touch came at a moment when everything seemed clouded with despair. Whenever it happened, there was one instant when God stooped down from heaven and kissed their owie and made it all better.

The real power of God is manifested in the fact that He doesn't do it with great fanfare and hoopla. He does it quietly and without fuss. It is a gift from Him to us. The tender ministration of a parent, doing at once no more and no less than expected. It is an intimate moment that we will treasure forever.

There was a time Joshua stopped coming to me to have his owies kissed. When he got to the ripe old age of 5 he decided that he was too old for that sort of thing. Rachel, however, is just discovering the intense power of a mother's kiss. I hope she and you and I never forget what it can do. And if we at times think, like Joshua, that we have outgrown such babyish doings I hope that we will catch a fleeting remembrance of the incredible power that is ours simply for the asking.

KISSING OWIES

Chapter 25

IF I HAD BEEN GOD

FOR GOD SO LOVED THE WORLD that he gave his one and only Son, that whoever believes in him shall not perish but have eternal life. John 3:16.

I was nursing him when I noticed that his breathing sounded like radio static, hissing in and out with a crackle and pop. He'd had a cold and was a little feverish, but I hadn't been too concerned until now. This did not sound good. At all.

I was able to get an appointment right away at the doctor's, and after a respectable wait the doctor bustled in. He examined Josh and asked me questions. Wrapping his stethoscope around his neck, he turned to me.

"Doesn't sound too good in there, but I can't be sure if it's pneumonia without an X-ray. I want you to take him to the hospital to get one."

I blinked at him in confusion. Joshua was 9 months old. Wasn't pneumonia really bad for a 9-month-old baby? He just didn't seem that sick. He wasn't eating well and he threw up sometimes when he coughed, but pneumonia? Didn't people go to the hospital for that? I gathered Joshua into my arms and pressed him against my chest to still my pounding heart.

At the hospital we waited in the lonely hallway for more than 45 minutes. Joshua was content to watch the orderlies and nurses, even though he had missed his morning nap and his breakfast. I clutched him tightly and worried.

When it was finally our turn in the X-ray room, I expected that they would let me stay near Josh while they took the X-ray. Instead, they asked me to step behind a partition while they strapped him into a plastic sleeve that forced him to keep his arms above his head, and turned him to face a wall. Agonizing moments passed like entire lifetimes. Joshua had no idea what they were doing to him, and he couldn't see me. He started to cry, and I joined him.

To keep myself from racing into the X-ray room and snatching him out of that contraption, I hugged my arms around myself so hard it made them hurt. The moment they unstrapped the plastic sleeve I pulled him into my arms. Immediately he buried his face in my shoulder as we shook and cried.

"It's OK," the technician assured me. "It didn't hurt him."

"I know, I know," I told her. But it had hurt me.

They left us alone as they went to develop the X-rays, and I held my son, my *only* son. In that moment I felt a rush of love that overwhelmed me. "O, Lord," I breathed, "what have You done to me? How can I love someone so much?"

I knew in that instant that if I had been God I wouldn't have let my Son come anywhere near earth if I thought He would so much as get a paper cut; forget about the atrocities that God knew would be committed against Him. If I had known my Son would be beaten, mistreated, misunderstood, and killed, I'm sorry, but earth would have been on its own.

IF I HAD BEEN GOD

If I had been God, nothing could have convinced me otherwise. I'm glad I was not God.

I read a gripping, fictitious story that went something like this: There was an outbreak of a virus. It quickly spread until the whole earth was infected. Scientists scrambled to find a cure. People were quarantined. Finally they began testing un-infected people for antibodies.

They tested your son and came back with the good news. They had found antibodies. In order to save the planet they would need your son's blood. All of it. Your son would have to die so that the rest of mankind might live. Would you do it? Would you let them take all of your son's blood so that the sick people on earth would live? Would you sacrifice your son? What if he were your only son?

It's possible for me, in an idealistic fit, to entertain the idea that, if there were no other choice, I would say yes, I would do this. But I know in my heart that I couldn't. It's just not possible. I've been in that emotional cubicle before. I felt the answer to that question. I couldn't do it.

What if God hadn't been able to do it, either?

"Son, I just can't allow You to do that."

"But, Father, I'm willing."

"I know You're willing, Son, and I'm proud of You. But think of the pain. Not only the physical pain, but the emotional torment. We'll be separated. *Separated.* We've never been sep-arated before. I'm not sure I could handle that. Could You?"

Jesus swallows hard. "It wouldn't be easy," He admits. "But I love You and I trust You and I know that We will be together again someday. I want to do this. I want to save them."

"Why?"

"Because I love them."

"You'll always look like them, You know. Forever. You'll

carry scars. Some they will be able to see, but the worst ones they won't. The ones on the outside will remind them to ask about the ones on the inside. You'll never be able to forget what happens down there, and neither will they."

"But it will make us closer," Jesus says. "It will make us brothers."

"How can I let You go?" God cries, pounding His chest. "How can I let them abuse You?"

"How can You not?" Jesus replies simply.

"I can't," God sighs finally. "I can't let You go."

Is that what He said? Not on your life. He said yes!

Later, in a damp garden, Jesus clings to a mossy rock and groans in agony. "Not My will, but Yours. If You can make this go away, if You can figure out some other way, please do it. But if You can't, then help Me to get through it. It is hard. So very hard."

And if God could have reached down from behind the partition of heaven and snatched His Son from the cruel earth He would have done it. But *because He loves us and because Jesus loves us,* They endured the agony and shame of His life and death here so that we could be with Them there forever.

That's love. That's what true love is. It is self-sacrificing, not to the point of resentment, but to the point of surrender. Popular songs and the media would like us to believe that love is a sappy feeling that comes and goes. But it's not. Love is an action, not a feeling. Good is a feeling. Warm is a feeling. But love is an action. Love is a choice.

It's something you choose to do for someone else, even if it is at your own expense. And because you love them it makes you happy to do it. If it makes you resentful then you aren't doing it out of love. You've got some other reason going on that you may not be aware of.

God loved us to the point of death. He held back nothing,

absolutely nothing, that could save us. What an awesome sacrifice. And yet, daily we ignore it, scoff at it, make light of it. We don't take His sacrifice seriously. We don't begin to realize what it cost.

If it had been your son . . . what would you have done?

I CALL HIM ABBA

Chapter 26

I LOVE MY MOM

THROUGH JESUS, THEREFORE, let us continually offer to God a sacrifice of praise—the fruit of lips that confess his name. Hebrews 13:15.

I admit it. Sometimes I am less than perfect. I know that statement will shock most people who don't know me well. I say that very tongue-in-cheek for those who really *don't* know me well, but it's true, nonetheless.

I am a confirmed introvert. Being around people (even my two little cherubs) for a long enough stretch without a break makes me cranky. Add to that the fuel of two children making equal but opposite demands simultaneously in relentless staccato, and *kaboom!* You have a mom in a snit, as Rob says.

Being older, Joshua picks up on these times with the sensitivity of a bloodhound tracking a particularly fresh trail. In his role as town crier he will announce my state of mental distress to the world. "My mom is crabby today!" is the usual pronouncement.

I don't know about you, but the last thing I want to hear

when I'm crabby is that I'm crabby. Particularly, I do not want to hear this from my 5-year-old son, who knows more, in his own estimation, than Aristotle and Einstein put together. It just makes me—well, crabbier.

One day I was rushing for a publisher's deadline and had several other projects crashing around my head, as well as Joshua and Rachel in full cry.

"Can you *wait?!* Just for a minute?" I snapped finally.

"My mommy is crabby," Joshua sang again and again. What could I say? He was right.

I sighed heavily. "Look, I'll do something with you guys in just a minute. Just let me finish this, OK?"

"Can we paint?" he asked thoughtfully, maneuvering like a lawyer.

"Sure," I agreed. "We can paint."

"I love my mommy. I love my mommy. Even when she's crabby," he sang happily. "I love you, Mom," he said, throwing his arms around my waist and snuggling his face against me.

Shame hit me like a tsunami.

How could I be crabby to such a sweet child? What was wrong with me? Somebody was going to take my mommy license away from me at this rate. But I had to question his child-like ability to sing about how much he loved me even when I was crabby. How often was I able to do that with God when things weren't going my way?

I shuddered to think about it.

"Abba, is it really Your will that the furnace, the water pump, and the woodstove all develop problems at the same time? Thanks, I love You."

"My dog ran away again. Thanks, I love You."

"How do You expect me to do Your work if my computer is dead? Thanks, I love You."

Sounds silly, doesn't it?

Paul didn't think so. "Give thanks in all circumstances, for this is God's will for you in Christ Jesus" (1 Thess. 5:18), he said.

It all boils down to contentment. I can't even claim the excuse of being cooped up with my kids too long. Paul lived under house arrest for two years when he wrote, "I have learned to be content whatever the circumstances. I know what it is to be in need, and I know what it is to have plenty. I have learned the secret of being content in any and every situation, whether well fed or hungry, whether living in plenty or in want" (Phil. 4:11, 12).

Content in *any* and *every situation?* Content when my children are bickering? Content when I'm cleaning up after my increasingly senile dog? Content when my husband is grouchy? Content facing surgery? So content, even, that I can praise God for allowing my circumstances?

Wouldn't you give a million dollars to know that secret? Seriously, how much would it be worth to you to be content *no matter what happened?* Can you imagine anything more valuable in this life? I can't.

Think about it. You could have money, but if you weren't content what good would it do you? You could have the most attractive, personable spouse, and darling, well-behaved offspring on the planet, but if you weren't content would you really enjoy them? You could have fame and recognition, but if you weren't content—you get the picture.

Fortunately, Paul doesn't leave us hanging. He tells us. He actually tells us. Here's a secret that could be mass marketed for millions and he gives it to us. For free!

Are you ready for this?

"I can do everything through him who gives me strength" (verse 13).

You know the sad thing? We read that with our eyes but it comes across as, "He can do all things for me with His strength." We take ourselves right out of that sentence, thereby releasing ourselves of responsibility. As a result, we sit around tapping our fingers on the table, waiting for Him to do it all. And when He doesn't we're . . .

Not content. Exactly.

Then we get crabby and our sons sing songs about us.

Of course, there is a catch. You knew there had to be, didn't you? All the power of the universe is at our disposal. We can use *all* of it if we need to. The only catch is that we have to ask for it. That's all. Just ask.

Think of it like banking. You have a limitless bank account (really!). You can write as many checks as you want. You never have to worry about being overdrawn. But you have to write the check. Or all the money stays in the bank. You can't factor out our responsibility in this transaction. We have to write the check. Personally. Signed with our very own signature.

Simple, isn't it?

It is when you consider the consequences of shoplifting, which is what we do when we try to get by without asking for God's help. We don't need to steal the merchandise or make do with the old stuff we have on hand. We can literally shop until we drop and never run out of resources. What are you waiting for?

Chapter 27

LIFE'S CHANGING FACE

HE HAS MADE EVERYTHING BEAUTIFUL in its time. He has also set eternity in the hearts of men; yet they cannot fathom what God has done from beginning to end. Ecclesiastes 3:11.

When I was a little girl I remember looking forward to the future. I could see changes and I anticipated them. Someday in my rosy future I would get married. I would have my own job (i.e., my own money so I could buy whatever I wanted). I would have all the horses I could ever want. And I would have children. A whole houseful of them.

It didn't dawn on me until much later that not only did things not turn out exactly the way you expect them to, but that even pleasant changes are accompanied by unpleasant changes. I enjoy having a husband, but I don't enjoy the times when we go to my parents' house and all my sisters are gone because *they've all grown up too.* That wasn't part of my plan. Nothing at home was supposed to change.

I love having my children crowd around the dinner table

when my extended family gets together for meals, but I don't like the fact that they fill up the empty spaces left by my grandfather, who passed away, and my grandmother, who alternates between the nursing home and the hospital. The table wasn't supposed to even out, it was supposed to *expand*.

I don't like people missing from Christmas celebrations because one sister lives in South Korea now and another travels a lot. I'm not happy that the Thanksgiving table is whittled down to so few faces when it used to barely hold all of us. I don't like changing traditions, even to make way for new ones.

My heart squeezes tight when I see Josh's face light up in anticipation of Christmas. But as he talks about all he's looking forward to I feel wistful, remembering that this stage of life is over for me. There won't ever be another time when I will look forward to the arrival of Christmas with such innocence and wonder. For me it will never be new again.

Glancing backward, I see what will never be again. So many things that I blithely took for granted before are changed forever. No amount of wishing will bring them back. Sometimes I wonder why I didn't appreciate them when I had them.

Eve must have done that, I think. Sitting around the campfire outside of Eden. Maybe heavy with the burden of her first child. She might have wrapped her arms around herself, trying to stay warm as she looked off into the night. The glow from the cherubim's sword flashed through the darkness from the direction of Eden. A profound sadness washed over her.

Recalling the evenings spent in the garden, walking with God, playing tag with the animals, brought sharp pangs of regret. That part of her life was over. If only she had realized how short-lived it was going to be, she would have appreciated it so much more! Her memories were bittersweet at best.

Even a hearty thump from within her growing abdomen did

little to dispel the cloud of remorse that smothered her. It was true, the new life was something to look forward to. It was a way of beginning again. But it also marked a distinction between her past and her future. The trouble was that she wasn't ready to let go of her past yet. She longed to savor it just one more season.

Her descendant Jacob probably had similar feelings as he fled all he held dear. Chances are that he was not ready to leave his mother's table, to let go of all the familiar things of childhood. A sensitive person, he would have been reluctant to leave them under the best of circumstances, in which he could return whenever he pleased to hold fast to what, overnight, became his past.

Forced to flee, he left behind his entire heritage that night. He abandoned all the homey customs that were so dear to him. He would never again taste his mother's cooking or watch his brother repair his hunting instruments by the light of the evening fire. He wouldn't hear his father's stories or tend his favorite animals. All of this was lost in the flight of one night. But you can be sure those memories returned again and again to tug at his heartstrings.

How many times must he have wept bitter tears, knowing that the entire way of life as he knew it was over? He couldn't go back. So he started over. And with his own children and his own family I'm sure he built on the traditions of his parents, and maybe added some of his own.

Then one day the impossible happened. He was able to go home after all. Of course, everything was different. His parents were dead, his brother grown and a powerful man in his own right. Even though he was able to return physically to the land where he grew up, still he never was able to capture the life that he missed so much. It was over.

It's true what they say. You can't go back. But you can go forward.

May I paint a picture for you?

Since we tend to think rather selfishly, we often forget that there was Someone else who felt the same pangs as Eve. Someone walked in the garden that same night. Silent tears rolled down His cheeks as He looked through the opening of the garden, past the cherubim, and saw the light flickering from her campfire.

His pain was unfathomable as He contemplated the perfection that was gone for those outside the garden. And even though He had done nothing wrong, He suffered as well. All the hopes and dreams He had had for Adam and Eve were shattered in one ugly moment. And this wasn't the first time.

Even before, happiness in heaven had been shattered by Lucifer's rebellion. Now, as angels gathered around His throne, blending their golden voices, He keenly missed the third that were missing. Never again would they all come together and sing their exquisite melodies. There was a distinct separation: past and present.

As He lingered on the paths in the garden, straining to catch a whisper of Adam or Eve's voice, He didn't dwell solely on the past. Because there was something more. There was something that made the situation tolerable. He could see into the future. He knew what was coming. He knew that ultimately those around His banquet table would rejoice. They would create new traditions. Sing new songs. They would begin again in the perfection of heaven and sin would be no more.

Ever.

I CALL HIM ABBA